TIBETAN WISDOM *for* MODERN LIFE

JOSEPH ARPAIA, M.D.
LOBSANG RAPGAY, PH.D

MOTILAL BANARSIDASS PUBLISHERS
PRIVATE LIMITED • DELHI

First Indian Edition: Delhi, 2004

(First published by Beyond Words Publishing, Inc., Hillsboro, Oregon, USA)

ISBN: 81-208-1941-1 (Cloth)
ISBN: 81-208-1955-1 (Paper)

MOTILAL BANARSIDASS
41 U.A. Bungalow Road, Jawahar Nagar, Delhi 110 007
8 Mahalaxmi Chamber, 22 Bhulabhai Desai Road, Mumbai 400 026
236, 9th Main III Block, Jayanagar, Bangalore 560 011
120 Royapettah High Road, Mylapore, Chennai 600 004
Sanas Plaza, 1302 Baji Rao Road, Pune 411 002
8 Camac Street, Kolkata 700 017
Ashok Rajpath, Patna 800 004
Chowk, Varanasi 221 001

Printed in India
BY JAINENDRA PRAKASH JAIN AT SHRI JAINENDRA PRESS,
A-45 NARAINA, PHASE-I, NEW DELHI 110 028
AND PUBLISHED BY NARENDRA PRAKASH JAIN FOR
MOTILAL BANARSIDASS PUBLISHERS PRIVATE LIMITED,
BUNGALOW ROAD, DELHI 110 007

contents

foreword

Training the mind is a steady process of familiarization. In the Buddhist context, such familiarization or meditation refers to the positive transformation of the mind, to the elimination of its defective qualities and the improvement of its positive qualities. Through meditation, we can train our minds in such a way that its negative qualities are abandoned and the positive qualities are generated and enhanced. In general, we talk about two types of meditation: analytical and single-pointed. First, the object of meditation is put through a process of analysis in which we repeatedly attempt to gain acquaintance with the subject matter. When we have gained confidence about the object of meditation, the mind is made to concentrate on it without further analysis. This combination of analytical and concentrative meditation is an effective technique for properly training the mind.

The importance of this practice arises from the fundamental fact that each and every one of us innately desires happiness and does not want misery. These are natural human characteristics that do not have to be created afresh. Happiness or sorrow in life depend largely on the state of our minds. And how the experiences we encounter affect our lives also depends on the mind. When we misuse our mental potential, we make mistakes and suffer unpleasant consequences. On the other hand, when the mind's potential is skillfully harnessed, we derive positive and pleasant results. Similarly, because of the control they have over their minds, some people are little disturbed by failure or adverse circumstances. This is a clear example of why training the mind is so important.

The authors of this book, Joseph P. Arpaia and Lobsang Rapgay, have drawn on both the Tibetan Buddhist traditions of meditation and the understanding of Western cognitive psychology, to try to present meditative practice in a way that readers will find is actually effective. I congratulate them for their efforts, and offer my prayers that readers who employ these techniques will indeed be successful in increasing a sense of peace and happiness in their own lives, and thereby contributing to greater peace and happiness in the world at large.

—His Holiness the Dalai Lama

THE DALAI LAMA

acknowledgments

From Lobsang:

I would like to acknowledge the infinite kindness of my root teacher, the late Junior Teacher to HH Dalai Lama, Kyabche Trichang Rinpoche, and the love and devotion of my late father, Karma Wangchuk Sherpa. I would also like to thank Dr. Herbert Benson, M.D., for his mentoring, and Sandy Thurman, Director, White House Office of National AIDS Policy, for her support and friendship.

From Joe:

I would like to thank the many teachers, students, and friends who I have known over the years, especially: Robert Bowman, Casey Carter, Andrew Elliott, Jim Elliott, Eugene and Kenny Friedrich, Fr. Joseph Glynn, Don Hoffman, Lee and Tina Kiester, Bud and Georgie Moore, Christine Padesky, Chagdud

Tulku Rinpoche, Curt Sandman, Don Schafer, Robert Shoemaker, Gery Souza, Jan Stafl, Deborah Stewart, and Judy Watkins.

A deep thanks to my wife, Marieke, for the years of love and companionship that we have shared, and to my daughters, Tia and Kerani, for their joy and exuberance.

Finally, I thank the spirit of love and mystery that is beyond all concepts and descriptions.

From both:

Both of us would like to thank the staff at Beyond Words Publishing, especially Richard Cohn and Cynthia Black, for working so closely and smoothly with us during the editorial process.

Peace to all beings.

introduction

What is your deepest desire? This may seem like a strange question to ask, but in our work with men and women from all walks of life, with myriad goals and difficulties, one common theme has emerged: people want peace, deep peace—a state of inner peace in which they feel complete, whole, and connected.

Yet these same people are caught up in the intense, frantic pace of Western life. They have spouses, children, bills, deadlines, performance reviews, and taxes. They are running families, departments, and companies. The pace of their life grows faster and faster. Peace seems to be ever more out of reach.

In this book, we introduce an extraordinary system of personal growth and transformation. It is extraordinary because it can enable you to find inner peace while staying in the fast lane of modern life; to maintain all of your responsibilities, and yet feel even more in control of them than before. You can live at an intense pace without becoming frantic, and actually find peace in the process!

This system is also extraordinary because anyone can use it. You do not have to belong to a particular religious tradition or follow an unusual way of life. You must simply be willing to learn to use your mind more effectively, and to spend an average of fifteen to twenty minutes per day doing so.

What we teach is extraordinarily practical. The system that you learn from this book will make a difference in your daily life. You will have more energy, think more clearly, and solve difficulties more creatively. After explaining some of the general principles that underlie our system, we teach you basic techniques to develop specific mental qualities, and show you how to use these techniques to improve your health, performance, relationships, and spiritual life.

WHO IS IT FOR? WHAT WILL IT DO?

We wrote this book for a wide audience. Those who have never meditated will find the instructions straightforward and easy to understand. Those who used to meditate but stopped for some reason will find a fresh perspective and numerous tips for making meditation work more effectively this time. And those who currently meditate will find a clear explanation of principles that can deepen and enhance their current practice.

Over the years, the people who we have taught, both beginners and those with prior experience, have reported numerous benefits. Some examples of these benefits follow.

HEALTH

- Feeling more energized
- Relief from minor ailments (such as headaches, indigestion, and insomnia)

- Reduced anxiety and depression
- Better eating and exercise habits, leading to weight loss

PERFORMANCE

- Accomplishing more at work and feeling less tired
- Decreasing golf handicap by five strokes in one month
- Increasing efficiency by 25 to 30 percent
- Finding creative solutions to problems at work

RELATIONSHIPS

- Going from "It's over!" to "It's good!"
- Increased communication, especially on difficult issues
- Finding freedom while staying close
- Better dialogue with teenage children

SPIRITUALITY

- Feeling love as a physical presence
- Discovering a source of inner wisdom
- Finding meaning in daily life
- Deepening one's own religious practice

WHAT WE OFFER

We call what we teach a system of meditation because it is derived from principles common to both Eastern and Western meditative systems. We found these principles to be most extensively described in the Tibetan Buddhist tradition.

When most Westerners hear of meditation, they think of Eastern religions, sitting still in strange postures, eliminating thoughts, and fasting for days. They believe meditation is something unusual that involves strange and uncomfortable practices.

This is completely wrong! Meditation is no more unusual than physical exercise. In fact, it is exercise for your mind. Fifty years ago, physical exercise was considered unusual: athletes exercised, but not ordinary people. No one jogged or went to the gym for fun fifty years ago. It wasn't until we understood that physical exercise had numerous health benefits (like reducing the chance of heart disease) that more people began to exercise.

Meditation is simply exercise for the mind, and it will benefit you in numerous ways. It will develop your mind so that you can perceive, think, and imagine better. It will enable you to feel emotions and understand them, so that you can respond instead of react. When you meditate correctly, you harmonize your body, mind, and spirit.

You do not need to flee to a monastery or scale the Himalayas to learn to meditate. Nor do you need to fast or punish yourself in order to benefit from meditation. True, people in monasteries fast for days at a time, or sit still for long periods while being bitten by mosquitoes. But they must challenge themselves with those discomforts because they don't have bills to pay or children to raise. It is far easier to fast for a week than to go to work every day while simultaneously taking care of your wife and children when they are sick. Sitting still and meditating while being bitten by mosquitoes is trivial when compared to sitting still and meditating while being bitten by worries about paying next month's bills.

The intense, hectic modern world is an excellent training ground for personal and spiritual growth. Instead of blooming in the greenhouse of a monastery, you can use meditation to express your inner peace like a wildflower in an alpine meadow. Instead of being beaten down by the pace of modern life, you can take the pressures that you experience and use them to energize yourself, and to propel yourself forward.

HOW WE GOT STARTED

Now that we have outlined some of the benefits of meditation, we would like to introduce ourselves and explain how our desire to make meditation accessible to Westerners brought us together and led to our collaboration on this book.

Lobsang speaks:

I was born in Lhasa, Tibet; the fourth in a family of nine children. When I was only four years old, we fled the Chinese Communists, like thousands of other Tibetans, and escaped into India. As a child, I remember the sadness I felt at the misery and poverty of my fellow Tibetans, as they streamed across the Indian border. Sometimes I would turn my head away to hide my grief and helplessness. I wanted to help them, and was fortunate to get accepted into a Catholic private school in India, where I received an excellent education.

When I was twenty years old, my father died. I decided to become a Buddhist monk, even though I had been schooled in a Western environment. I joined the Buddhist School of Dialectics for young Tibetan monks, started by His Holiness the Dalai Lama. There I studied the ancient texts and learned to debate, pray, and meditate. I took advanced teachings and training from my root gurus, Kyabche Trichang Rinpoche, the Tutor to His Holiness the Dalai Lama, and Khen Lati Rinpoche, the Abbot of Gaden Shartse Monastic College. Because I had both a Western education and a knowledge of Buddhist scriptures, I worked as a deputy secretary and translator for His Holiness the Dalai Lama.

I enjoyed this work greatly, but I also wanted to understand how the Western mind worked, and felt that studying psychology in the West would be the way to do so. I felt deeply that I could be of better service to His Holiness and the Tibetan people by pursuing this interest. I discussed this feeling with His Holiness, and he was very supportive of my position. Since coming to the United States, I have completed my studies and am now a staff psychologist and Assistant Clinical Professor in Psychiatry at UCLA, and a clinical instructor at Harvard Medical School. I balance my work as a monk and my position in Western society with the sincere hope that I can make life meaningful for my people, despite what has happened in Tibet.

Joseph speaks:

As a child, I often felt that there was a wonderful spiritual world of peace and love just on the other side of an invisible barrier. There were times when I would find myself on the other side of that barrier. I yearned to discover how to cross this barrier at will, and even how to live in both worlds at once. And I wanted to help other people do this, too.

Because I was raised as a Catholic, I naturally thought that this process of finding peace would involve becoming a priest. However, while I found plenty of structure in Catholicism and a loving spiritual presence, I found no tools for connecting with that presence. I was simply to follow the rules and perform the rituals. This did not satisfy me.

I received a smattering of meditation instruction when I started martial arts in high school, but no real training. My thirst for knowledge of such things did not begin to be satisfied until I attended college at CalTech. My scholastic focus was chemistry, and my meditative studies were strictly extracurricular. I practiced Zen for a couple of years, and then studied Christian contemplative prayer with a Carmelite priest. I learned that I was interested in more than simply finding a system of meditation to study. I wanted to know how meditation worked so that I could use it and teach it to others.

I continued to explore meditation through my years in college, medical school, and psychiatric training. By the time I became a psychiatrist, I had been practicing meditation for almost fifteen years. In addition to Zen and Christian contemplative prayer, I had studied Kundalini and Taoist Yoga, and had begun exploring Tibetan Buddhism. I had also studied psychology and mathematical theories of perception. Through my studies I came to believe that an integration of Eastern and Western ideas was vitally needed in modern society. It was at this point that I attended a talk at a small bookstore near Los Angeles. It was a gray winter evening, and the speaker was a Tibetan monk—Lobsang Rapgay.

When we met, we found that we shared a strong desire to integrate Eastern and Western spiritual systems. We also shared the experience of having met numerous people who wanted to change, but who did not know how. Many of these people had tried using meditation to make a positive change in their lives, but with disappointing results. Some of them thought meditation was just for relaxing; others had good experiences during meditation, but had no positive changes in their personality. Some were confused by the techniques, and their practice was ineffective. We even met a few people who were negatively affected by meditation. These people had become more distant and removed, or they had stopped thinking for themselves and let their "guru" do that for them. Their ineffective use of meditation had made them unstable.

One of the problems that stood out was that Westerners seemed to adopt Eastern practices without understanding the meanings behind the practices. They would chant mantras in a strange language that they did not fully understand. Or they would attempt complex visualizations, without knowing what ideas were symbolized by the different elements of the visualized image. People often would have powerful emotional experiences while on retreats, but these would not cause positive transformations in their personalities when they returned home.

We were very disturbed by this phenomenon, because we knew that meditative systems had been designed to help people improve themselves. Furthermore, each of us had undergone powerful, personally transformative experiences with meditation. We knew that meditation had a lot more to offer than just relaxation, and that it should lead to positive changes in one's personality and in all areas of one's life.

The psychologist Carl Jung warned about the dangers of Westerners adopting meditation techniques directly from the East. He believed that cultural differences between East and West made it difficult for Westerners to benefit from practicing Eastern techniques; thus, Westerners needed more than simple translations of the Eastern texts. Jung said that eventually the West would develop its own yoga, its own science of mental and spiritual transformation that was as precise and as effective as anything in the East.

This book is a step toward that goal. For seven years, we met frequently and practiced many types and variations of meditation techniques. As we practiced, we talked about the effect that each technique had on our minds. We could sense and describe these effects with clarity and precision because each of us had expertise in both meditation and psychology. We eventually learned enough to explain the principles underlying the techniques in purely Western terms.

As we worked together, we found that small differences in the techniques could cause great differences in the effects on our minds. We noticed patterns in the relationship between the techniques and their effects. We discovered that we could describe the mental effects of the techniques by referring to five basic mental qualities. As we looked deeper, we realized that our experience could be precisely explained by drawing on ideas from the Tibetan Buddhist system. We then developed a system of meditation that integrates these Tibetan ideas with the Western outlook.

Investigating meditation is an extremely complex and personal process. Each of us began this task with his own extensive background of knowledge and experience. Considering our different backgrounds, our work together has been remarkably smooth.

From our dialogue at such a personal level, we have formed a friendship. This friendship is deep and meaningful, even though much of it is unspoken; somehow we connect at a nonverbal, intuitive level. We pick up each other's thoughts, and often finish each other's sentences. Even when discussing sensitive issues during the writing of this book, we could resolve our differences because of our mutual openness and respect for each other.

This mutual respect for each other's spiritual beliefs and training has enabled us to interact, not as a Westerner and an Easterner, but as two friends working as partners in a common endeavor. Lobsang was born into a Buddhist family in Tibet; Joe was born into a Catholic family in New York. An amazing string of coincidences brought us to work together in Los Angeles. We hope that our collaboration can lead you to a deep experience of inner peace that will stay with you throughout your life.

AN "INNER" PERSPECTIVE

Most of the activity in meditation is internal; it goes on inside of you. It is interesting work, exciting and often humorous. This inner activity of personal growth is not captured by lists of meditation instructions. The real excitement is illustrated by the inner activities of someone who is working on, sometimes struggling with, and eventually succeeding at the meditation practices.

In order to give the reader this perspective, we introduce Brian and Maria, whose stories we follow throughout the book. Brian and Maria are invented amalgams of the lives and personalities of hundreds of people that we have taught. You will watch Brian and Maria as they practice the basic techniques and their applications. You will observe the intimate details of their struggles and successes. As you observe Brian's and Maria's internal dialogues, you will have the closest possible view of the inner experience of someone engaged in personal growth through the practice of meditation.

As you read Brian's and Maria's experiences, you will find them remembering comments from their teacher. This teacher is meant to be either of the authors, and the teacher's comments appear in italics. These comments contain tips that you will find helpful as you work with the techniques yourself.

We used a man and a woman as examples because there are patterns that are more common in men and others that are more common in women. Brian will exhibit the typically male pattern and Maria will demonstrate the usual female pattern. Please remember, however, that individuals are unique. There are men who will relate more to Maria's experience, and there are women who will relate more to Brian's. The important point is that Brian and Maria together give a thorough picture of what it is like to practice meditation.

Brian's Story

Brian is a middle-aged married man with three children, ages seven to fourteen. He works full-time in a middle-management position.

Brian finds his job stressful, and his doctor thinks the stress is contributing to his neck tension and high blood pressure. Brian has difficulties with outbursts of anger that have a negative effect on his home life, especially with his teenage son. He feels an ongoing sense of conflict with the world, and carries himself with a tense, irritable attitude. Brian is not happy with himself, and he feels stuck, as though his life were becoming a dead end. He finds himself asking the question, "Is this all there is?" He would like to be different, but he has no idea of what to do. Everything seems to be out of his control. At times he feels sad and even hopeless. His doctor has suggested that he might be clinically depressed.

One day, while talking to his sister, Karen, a nurse, he expressed his frustration. At one point in their conversation she looked at him very seriously and asked, "Are you willing to put some time and effort into changing, and do you have the patience?"

Brian was surprised by her intensity, but replied, "I need to do something. There is no crisis yet, but if things keep going the way they are, they will get worse."

"Well then," she replied, "I suggest you start meditating."

"What?" Brian exclaimed. "How is sitting around staring at my navel going to help me? I've tried relaxation and stress-reduction, and they don't work for me."

"Look, Brian," she said, "you said you wanted a change. I'm telling you about something that will change you, more than you can imagine. Meditation is a lot more than relaxation or staring at your navel."

"I don't have time to meditate," he complained.

"Athletes and businessmen have used meditative techniques to become more effective. If they can make the time, then so can you. Or," his sister stated bluntly, "if you don't want to do that, maybe you can try Prozac."

Brian drew a deep breath. "Thanks for being straight, sis. So what do I do? Where do I learn meditation?"

"There is an introductory session being held by a teacher I know," his sister replied. "I suggest you attend that. When you go, make sure you ask any questions you have. If meditation is going to work for you, it will need to make sense. So if something doesn't sound right, ask about it."

Maria's Story

Maria is a young married woman with two small children. She also has a full-time job outside the home as an administrative assistant. She is being given more responsibilities at work and wants to move ahead there, but her family also takes a lot of energy. Balancing her work and home responsibilities is stressful, and Maria is starting to suffer the effects. She is having headaches, feels tired a lot, and is losing her patience too often.

Over the past couple of months, Maria has been feeling scattered and overstressed. She feels like a rat running on a treadmill, with someone continually increasing the speed. It is taking all her energy just to keep up. There are so many demands on her attention that she feels overwhelmed. Her headaches have gotten worse, and her doctor has prescribed medicine for them; the medicine helps decrease the pain, but it also sedates her. The sedation increases her feelings of being scattered and unable to keep up.

One day she had lunch with an older friend and admitted, "Well, Susan, I just don't know. There is so much to do: the kids, my job, the household, my husband. It keeps piling up. I feel more and more scattered and stressed-out. I wish I could keep up and stay organized like you do."

Susan looked at her thoughtfully and said, "My secret to keeping up with everything is that I meditate. It's something you might try."

"But I don't have the time to meditate every day," Maria replied.

"I don't meditate every day. I meditate three times a week."

"But I don't even have time for that," Maria complained.

"If you meditate and become more efficient, you may actually gain more time than you spend," Susan replied. "For example, if you were able to reduce the amount of headache medicine you needed, you wouldn't experience the sedation that slows you down so much."

"Meditation can help my headaches?"

"People who practice meditation often have improvements in their physical ailments," Susan stated.

"But I'm a Christian and meditation is a Buddhist thing," Maria argued.

"Meditation is a mental thing," Susan responded. "Its about learning to use your mind. Christians have been meditating for almost two thousand years."

"But aren't you supposed to get rid of all your thoughts and experience nothingness by blanking out your mind?" Mary asked.

"No. Not at all. It's certainly not what I do when I meditate. Meditation has helped me a lot and I think it will be very helpful for you. I suggest you go to an introductory session and ask the teacher your questions."

Maria was skeptical, but she respected her friend and knew that Susan was a very stable, practical person. She decided to attend the introductory session, and see how she felt about it afterward.

HOW TO USE THIS BOOK

This book is much more than a list of instructions. It is also a story that will guide you into the experience of personal growth and inner peace. Though we advise you to practice the techniques in the order that we present them, we also encourage you to read ahead and find sections that interest you. You may wish to read the sections describing Brian and Maria in each chapter, and share in their difficulties and successes. You may also wish to look at the comments and tips from their teacher that appear in italics. Reading Brian's and Maria's stories will give you a feeling for the process that occurs when ordinary people train their minds and achieve extraordinary results.

PART ONE

FOUR PRACTICES FOR FIVE MENTAL QUALITIES

one

what is meditation anyway, and what's in it for me?

Look far ahead,
Be farsighted,
Be in tune.

Meditation is not merely a calming exercise. It is an active process that is specifically designed to develop a number of mental skills. First, the meditator learns to be alone and centered. Once centered, the meditator strengthens the cognitive skills of attention, awareness, and concentration. Each of these skills produces a certain amount of tranquility, however tranquility is not the final goal. The meditator must use the skills to yoke the analytical and emotional parts of the mind to the task of transforming negative emotions into love and compassion. As the task of transformation is carried out, the meditator harnesses the primitive instinctive forces of the psyche and is propelled into the depths of the unconscious. There, the meditator uncovers the clear light, the natural state of the mind, and uses it for liberation. Throughout this process, the meditator must maintain the right level of effort, neither too intense, nor too relaxed.

—Geshe Karag Gomchung

THE RESULTS OF MEDITATION

An elderly man, grimacing in intense pain, closes his eyes. Soon, the grimace fades, his breathing deepens, and he relaxes comfortably into the sofa. A runner, slowed by advancing years, says his legs now feel twenty years younger. A young executive, troubled by anger, no longer explodes when her buttons are pushed. A mother, wracked by guilt, experiences love and compassion for herself and those she lives with.

We have taught these people, and many like them, to benefit quickly from practicing and applying meditation. The specific application techniques differ among people: the elderly gentleman, the runner, the executive, and the mother were all using different techniques. However, those different techniques were all based on identical principles; principles based on everyday experience, and which we describe in simple and intuitive terms. What happens when you blend these techniques into daily life? Let us illustrate that with the following story.

It was a late evening in midwinter, and a young parent was driving home from work. It had been a long, hard day in a long, hard week. Thoughts hammered in his head. Worry and frustration gripped his stomach. As he squinted into the glare of oncoming headlights, he could feel unfinished work nagging at his mind, increasing the tension in his tired body. "Home and rest, home and rest," he thought.

When he pulled into his driveway, a small voice in his head reminded him of what he had forgotten during his drive to "get home and rest." The hour was late, and his children were waiting for him in a frenzy of anticipation. They would want his attention and be upon him in a clamor.

Other thoughts rose up: "Its not fair!... I need space and time to unwind ... Doesn't anyone care?" Anger, frustration, and sadness spiraled upward in intensity. He tried to turn the emotions off, but with little success. He saw flashes of past incidents of which he was not proud; when his angry words and slammed doors had created fear in those he loved.

He took a deep breath and unclenched his teeth. His head was hurting, his stomach in knots, and he was radiating hurt, anger, and despair. He couldn't walk in the door like that. He allowed himself to sit back in the car seat and closed his eyes. His mind raised a protest, "You're late getting home. You can't just sit here in the driveway, you need to get inside!" His body immediately became even more tense. He took a deep breath and thought about that protest. It was ridiculous. Clearly, it made no sense to hurry inside in his current state. Time spent becoming peaceful was time well spent.

He focused his mind on a well-practiced thought pattern. "Calm—relaxed," he said to himself. He repeated this thought, "calm—relaxed," over and over. Thoughts of work intruded and caught his attention, but he simply returned to thinking "calm—relaxed." His breathing became easier, the tightness in his temples and the knots in his stomach dissolved. As he noticed these effects, he had a brief fear that he would not be able to keep them up; that the pain and tension would return. He noted the fear, identified it as "fear," and went back to his focus on "calm—relaxed."

Now he was calmer and his body had sunk into the car seat. The tension in his stomach was gone; the headache, however, remained threatening. He changed thought patterns to deal with it. "Arms warm and heavy," he repeated to himself, over and over. His body relaxed even more, and the headache receded as he became increasingly aware of a wonderfully pleasant warmth in his palms. He let go even of the thought "arms warm and heavy," and just enjoyed breathing peacefully, feeling more and more comfortable with each breath. Thoughts of work were few and fleeting now. He could see that all the critical tasks had been done, and he could accept the fact that there would always be unfinished work.

Now he was ready to change roles. He would let go of the work role and move into the new role that was needed. He smiled as he thought about his children and how much he cared about them. His mind deliberately focused on memories of their laughter and joy, evoking the loving emotions associated with them. As he did so, he felt his body change to resonate with those positive feelings. A couple of breaths later and he could feel those positive emotions permeating him from head to toe.

He opened his eyes, a smile on his face and crinkles of laughter around his eyes. Less than ten minutes had been required to make the change. No longer was he a harried refugee from the rat race. As he walked to the door with a light step and a smile on his face, now he was just Dad.

These are the kinds of results that you can expect from practicing the techniques in this book. You will learn four basic meditative practices that are built on a logical system of principles. You will then learn how to modify and combine those basic practices into useful applications. What is more, you will learn how to come up with your own combinations of techniques that are tailored for the situations in which you find yourself. In that way, you will be able to experience inner peace through the hustle and bustle of daily life.

MEDITATION = EXERCISE FOR THE MIND

You might be asking, "But what is meditation?" By "meditation" we are referring to mental exercises that improve the mind in the same way that physical exercises improve the body.

Athletes exercise because they have a goal in mind. They want to sprint faster, or swim farther, or do gymnastics better. They use specific exercises to improve physical qualities such as balance, speed, flexibility, and strength. As they improve these physical qualities, they naturally run, swim, and do gymnastics better.

In the same way, meditative exercises develop five primary mental qualities: *steadiness, pliancy, warmth, clarity*, and *spaciousness*. (We describe these qualities more fully later in this chapter). As you develop these mental qualities, you will find that your mind automatically performs tasks with greater ease. You become more adept at keeping calm under pressure, adapting to new situations, working through conflicts, and finding creative insights. You become better at living, not just at meditating.

Learning to meditate is like learning to ride a bicycle: When you start learning to ride the bicycle, you feel awkward and fall frequently. So you practice in your driveway, or on a quiet street. You accept the fact that you are going to fall, and you try various tricks to get better. As you practice, your skill improves. Soon you are falling less often, and can ride on busier streets. If you keep practicing, eventually you are able to ride anywhere while feeling safe, and are able to handle emergencies as they arise. But in order to learn, you first must be willing to try—and to risk falling. You must accept the fact that you will make mistakes, and you have to try different riding techniques in order to find one that works.

In the same way, when you start practicing meditation it is natural to feel awkward. You will experience varying degrees of success. Sometimes you will see positive results, and other times you will feel like you are just sitting and getting nowhere. If you are patient with yourself, you will improve with practice.

Most people think meditation techniques require extended amounts of time, hours or even days. This misperception exists because meditative traditions were developed in monasteries and similar settings. The techniques developed in monasteries require a lot of time simply because monks and nuns have the time; they are supposed to spend hours meditating and praying. Those of us who have jobs or families do not have hour upon hour to spend meditating.

That is why we teach brief meditation techniques, as well as extended techniques. The extended techniques take between fifteen and thirty minutes. Their purpose is to give the experience of developing specific mental skills in an undisturbed setting. The brief techniques, on the other hand, require as little as ten seconds and no more than two minutes, and they are done throughout the day. Their purpose is to give you the experience of using your mental skills in real-life situations.

The brief techniques are critically important. They allow you to make progress without spending long periods of time sitting in meditation. While the extended techniques develop mental qualities and help you to experience peace, the brief techniques make it possible for you to remain peaceful throughout the day. When you practice the brief techniques, you are using meditation in the real world.

PRACTICE TIPS

In this section, we give you some tips that will help you learn to meditate. If you follow these guidelines, you will feel more comfortable practicing meditation and you will see results more quickly.

EXTENDED TECHNIQUES

Extended meditation sessions are what most people picture when they think of meditation. Extended meditation sessions last at least fifteen minutes. You will need to spend a total of at least ninety minutes per week in extended sessions to make progress. You could practice fifteen minutes per day, six days per week. Or, you could practice thirty minutes per day every Monday, Wednesday, and Friday. Try not to let more than two days pass between sessions.

If you spend more time in the extended meditation sessions, you will progress faster, but only up to a point. If you meditate thirty minutes per day six days per week, you will progress about twice as fast as if you practiced fifteen minutes per day; if you practice forty-five minutes per day, you will progress about three times as fast. We advise that you not spend more than forty-five minutes per day in extended meditation sessions. The techniques in this book are not appropriate for longer amounts of time, and spending more than forty-five minutes per day in extended sessions will not improve your progress.

As much as possible, try to practice the extended meditation sessions in the same place, at the same time of day, and in the same posture. Doing so helps the extended sessions become a habit. Pick a place that has a comfortable temperature and few disturbing noises. Good times to practice are early morning after waking, lunch hour, just after work, or late evening. Sit or lie in a posture that keeps your back straight and allows you to feel comfortable without falling asleep. One popular posture is to sit in a chair with your feet flat on the floor; another is to sit on a cushion on the floor with your legs crossed. A third is to kneel on a rug or carpet with your buttocks resting on your heels. Any posture is acceptable, as long as it allows you to stay upright and comfortable for at least fifteen minutes.

BRIEF TECHNIQUES

The more you practice the brief techniques, the faster you will make progress. You should practice the brief techniques during the "between-times": periods of time when you are not doing anything that requires your full attention. The following is a list of some of the between-times that we or our students have found for practicing the brief techniques:

- before and after meals
- just after waking up, unless you are about to do an extended session
- just before falling asleep, unless you have just finished an extended session
- while walking from one room to another
- while walking out to the car
- before driving or after driving
- while someone else is driving
- while going to the bathroom, (yes, really!)
- while washing up after going to the bathroom
- in the shower
- while waiting "on hold" during a phone call
- before picking up the newspaper or a magazine
- instead of picking up the newspaper or the magazine
- before or after reading a book on meditation (but not instead of reading the book)

If you use your creativity, you will find numerous intervals in your day in which to practice a brief technique. The more often you do this, the faster you will progress.

The following instructions apply to both the brief and the extended meditation techniques. Each of the techniques has three separate phases: *intention*, *execution*, and *reflection*. When most people think about meditation, they think only of the execution phase. The intention and reflection phases are also extremely important to remember, however, because they dramatically improve your progress.

The first phase, *intention*, is very quick. In this phase, you focus on the goals you have for meditation; what you want to accomplish. You think about your intended results. We can describe this best by using examples. Before a weightlifter attempts to perform a lift, he focuses his mind on his intended result, lifting the weight. Before a tennis player serves the ball, she focuses her mind on what she wants to accomplish, placing the ball at a certain place on the opposite court. Before a martial artist breaks a brick, he focuses his mind on his intended goal, directing a massive amount of energy through the brick. In these examples, the athletes focus their mind's intention, to improve their chance of success.

To focus your intention as you start a meditation technique, simply think about what you want to accomplish by meditating. Answer the question, "Why am I doing this?" If you are practicing meditation to improve your health, remind yourself of that. If you are meditating to become more loving, then think about that. You need only a couple of seconds, or less, to complete the intention phase. By focusing your intention at the beginning of each brief and extended practice session, you will learn much faster.

Once you have focused your intention, stop thinking about your goals, and begin to practice the technique for that session. This is the *execution* phase of the session. The execution phase takes the most time and is what people typically think of as "meditating." It is the phase in which most of the work of meditation occurs.

The last phase is that of *reflection*. Its purpose is to facilitate the integration of your experiences from the execution phase into your daily life. It is analogous to the "follow-through" described in athletic events. For the reflection phase, remain quiet and remember any experiences from the session that stand out in your mind. Think about how those might relate to the goals that you focused on during the intention phase of the session. This will take a couple of seconds after a brief meditation technique, and may take up to a minute after an extended session. Reflecting on your experiences will reinforce the mental processes related to your goals, and make the benefits of the meditation session easier to experience during the rest of the day.

TIME PRESSURE

The most common objection people raise to practicing meditation is that they do not have the time for it. Most people already feel too busy, and the thought of adding another activity to the day seems overwhelming.

Meditation is one of those things that is important but not urgent. It is like brushing your teeth. Nothing terrible will happen if you don't brush your teeth one night. However, if you don't brush them regularly, they will decay and fall out. (You will also lose a lot of friends.) You brush your teeth because you were trained to do so as a child. It became a habit, and now it feels good to have clean teeth. In the same way, you must make meditation a habit. When it becomes part of your daily routine, you will use the techniques instinctively as situations arise throughout the day.

One way to deal with the feeling of time pressure is to realize that it is a question of priorities. One student described how she was lying in bed, feeling reluctant to get up and practice, when the thought hit her, "You have a date with God and you're blowing Him off!" That got her meditating.

Another way of dealing with the time issue is to realize that we have a natural tendency to avoid changing our ways. We will underestimate the negative consequences of continuing as we have, and overestimate the negative consequences of changing. By misinterpreting the facts, our mind keeps us from improving; we stay stuck. This is illustrated by the following story, told by Joe.

One evening I was traveling to teach, of all things, a meditation class. I was delayed at my office and left later than I planned to, so I felt a lot of time pressure. The trip was a little over a hundred miles and usually took about two hours. I estimated that if I didn't have any delays from traffic, then I would arrive at the class with about five minutes to spare.

As I drove out of the parking lot, I noticed that my car was very low on fuel. However, I was feeling a lot of time pressure. My mind was saying, "Keep driving so you won't be late," and "You don't have time to get gas." So, I looked at the gas gauge closely and decided that I had enough fuel to get to my destination. As I drove toward the freeway I passed a gas station and realized that I could pull in quickly and fill my tank in just a couple of minutes. But my mind said, "Keep driving, you don't have time to get fuel."

As I traveled on the freeway, I kept glancing at my gas gauge. I began to wonder if I really had enough fuel. Maybe I was fooling myself about how much I actually had. I passed a couple of exits that had gas stations right by the freeway off-ramp, but I was still stuck in the "keep driving, you don't have time" pattern.

Finally, about halfway to my destination, I realized that there was no way I was going to make it without getting fuel. In fact, I was probably running on fumes by that time. Unfortunately, I was not in a place where there was a convenient gas station. I took the next exit and had to drive for a couple of miles before finding one. As I drove back to the freeway, I realized that I had wasted at least fifteen minutes by not refueling at the first gas station I passed when I started the trip.

Since I was now definitely running late, I felt even more time pressure. As I got near my destination, I realized that the directions I had were confusing me. My mind kept up the thought, "Keep driving, you're late, you don't have time to pull over and look at the map." Fortunately, I noticed these thoughts, and having been burned by that line of thinking already, I didn't pay attention to them. I pulled off to the side of the road and looked at my map. In less than two minutes I had reoriented myself and understood the directions. I was able to drive to the class without any further delays, and got there only about ten minutes late.

Often we run our lives the way Joe took that trip. We push ourselves and don't stop to recharge because we feel rushed, but that costs us much more time in the long run. Or, we may have plenty of energy, but we don't quite know how to direct it and end up pursuing activities that seem to get us nowhere.

Taking the time to meditate will keep you from falling into those traps. It strengthens your mind so that it runs like a car with a full tank of gas instead of one that is sputtering on an empty tank. It also clarifies your awareness of what is important, giving you an internal compass that helps you direct your energy effectively and efficiently.

FIVE MENTAL QUALITIES

As you practice the basic meditative exercises in this book, you naturally develop five primary mental qualities: *steadiness*, *pliancy*, *warmth*, *clarity*, and *spaciousness*. These mental qualities are active in everything your mind does. They help you perceive, remember, think, and imagine. They also help you react creatively and constructively to events that occur in daily life.

The first four mental qualities complement each other in pairs; steadiness and pliancy complement each other, as do warmth and clarity. Steadiness helps your mind stay focused, whereas its complement, pliancy, shifts your focus quickly and smoothly. Warmth helps you become more open and accepting, whereas its complement, clarity, helps you notice details and sharpens your analytical skills. The fifth mental quality, spaciousness, stands apart from and is complemented by the other four. Your mind functions most effectively when each quality is balanced by its complementary quality.

You can't have too much of any one of these mental qualities. But you can have an imbalance, and you correct the imbalance by developing what you lack. For example, if you have much steadiness and little pliancy, then you will be able to focus your mind on tasks easily. However, you will have difficulty changing your focus if the situation changes. The solution is not to decrease your steadiness and thus reduce your ability to focus. Instead, you should increase your pliancy so that you can both focus well and shift focus as needed.

Your mind uses these mental qualities constantly. We describe their activity in everyday situations, so that you can get a feel for how they work. You will also get a sense of which mental qualities you have in abundance, and which you need to strengthen.

Steadiness and Pliancy

Steadiness is the mental quality that helps you stay focused. It keeps your mind from wandering even in the presence of distractions. Mental steadiness is important because it has a stabilizing influence on your mind. When your mind is steady, you can maintain the focus of your awareness and thinking, as well as remain in emotional states that you wish to prolong. Mental steadiness is also important because it helps you move toward goals in a consistent manner. People who apply themselves to any protracted course of training, either physical or intellectual, have a highly developed mental steadiness.

Pliancy is the mental quality that helps your mind stretch and flow. While steadiness helps you stay on track, pliancy helps you to switch tracks when necessary. Mental pliancy is like flexibility in the body. When your body is flexible, you can move quickly and smoothly. When your mind is pliant, you can shift attention quickly and smoothly from one topic to another. You can also expand or contract your awareness to encompass whatever you wish to pay attention to. When your mind is pliant, your mental activity has a smooth flow that is relaxed and unhurried.

The following examples demonstrate how steadiness and pliancy complement each other. If you are playing tennis, you must keep your eye on the ball. You must also stay aware of both your position on the court and your opponent's position. While doing this, you must ignore all other distractions—for instance, worries about performance, or people watching you. Steadiness helps you to ignore distractions and keep track of the ball. Pliancy helps you to shift your awareness quickly and smoothly enough to keep track of your position and your opponent's position as well.

If you are driving, and wish to shift lanes at a busy freeway interchange, you must keep track of the car in front of you *and* look to the sides *and* in your mirrors to locate other cars. Pliancy helps you shift your attention rapidly from the front to the rear and both sides. It also helps you build a mental picture that includes the positions of the other cars in all directions. While you are shifting attention, steadiness helps you to keep track of the car in front of you, so that you can avoid hitting it if it stops suddenly.

If you are giving a complex speech to an important audience, it is normal to be anxious. It is also important to be able to focus on your talk. Steadiness helps your mind to stay focused despite your anxiety. If members of the audience ask questions, you may have to shift topics to respond effectively to the questions. Pliancy helps you shift smoothly from one topic to another without getting confused.

Steadiness and pliancy are also important in relationships. For example, if you have children and feel tired and anxious when you return home from work, you need to be able to shift into a playful mood so that you can interact well with your children. Pliancy helps you change from being anxious to being playful. Steadiness helps you continue to be playful even when thoughts of work begin to intrude. At other times, you might be upset with someone, but want to avoid an angry confrontation. Pliancy helps you disengage from your anger and shift into a neutral state. Steadiness helps you maintain that neutral state long enough to listen to the other person.

Steadiness and pliancy work together so that you can direct sustained attention and simultaneously keep track of other events. As you increase your steadiness and pliancy in a balanced manner, you will increase your ability to keep track of many tasks at once. You will be able to respond more easily to life's constant changes. Steadiness is developed by centering techniques taught in chapter 2. Pliancy is developed by attending techniques taught in chapter 3.

Warmth and Clarity

Warmth and clarity are the next complementary pair of mental qualities. Warmth is the quality that helps you to be open to the unexpected, and to accept things without prejudging them. It is directly related to tolerance and openness. Warmth allows your mind to accept things it would ordinarily reject automatically.

Clarity is the mental quality that helps your mind make distinctions and categorize. It helps you pick out details and distinguish one thing from another. It also increases your ability to analyze. A musician uses clarity to tune one instrument to another. A baseball umpire uses clarity to tell the difference between a ball and a strike. Clarity is most useful when you use it to notice the details of your own internal states; it helps you to know precisely what is on your mind.

Warmth and clarity work together in many situations. If you disagree with your spouse about something, you must be able to listen in an accepting manner even though you disagree. After all, until you have truly understood them, how can you disagree intelligently? Warmth helps you listen to the ideas and emotions that your spouse is communicating. Clarity helps you to understand the details of your spouse's statements and how they relate to the current situation.

Warmth and clarity are very important because they allow you to be aware of your thoughts, emotions, or impulses, especially those that may make you uncomfortable. If your teenage son comes home very late, you are likely to feel anger as he walks in the door. Warmth allows you to notice other emotions—for example, fear, disappointment, guilt, worry, or relief—that the anger might be masking. Clarity helps you to understand how these emotions relate to the current situation. You might feel afraid that your son could have been hurt. You might feel disappointed that he didn't have the courtesy to call. You might feel guilty about being an inadequate parent. You might feel worried that your son was becoming irresponsible. And you would probably feel relieved that he was safe. Warmth helps you accept all the emotions that you feel. Clarity helps you identify them precisely and understand their origin.

Sometimes, you feel an emotion that does not seem to have been caused by a specific event. When this happens, warmth helps you to be aware of all the sensations and thoughts that you usually ignore. Clarity helps you to separate these sensations and thoughts, and then evaluate their influence on your current mood. For example, if you are at work and the day is going reasonably well, you might find yourself feeling irritable, "for no reason." However, your irritation could come from a number of factors. You may not be getting things done as quickly as you'd like, or you may wish that you were on vacation, or you may have had an argument with your spouse that morning, or you may simply be hungry. Warmth helps you to be open to unexpected factors that are related to your irritability. Clarity helps you to see precisely how each factor relates to your irritability. As a result, you can decide whether you should settle for doing a little less at work that day, start planning a vacation that evening, call your spouse and apologize, or get something to eat.

Warmth and clarity help you to become more open to external and internal events. At the same time, they help you to notice the details of those events and understand how they are interrelated. As you increase your warmth and clarity in a balanced manner, you will increase your ability to analyze several perspectives at once. You will be more accepting of other's ideas and at the same time understand how to explain your own. Warmth is developed by attending techniques taught in chapter 3, and clarity is developed by concentrating techniques taught in chapter 4.

Spaciousness

Spaciousness is the mental quality that complements the other four. Spaciousness is experienced as a sense of freedom, of mental vastness. It is required for humor and creativity. When you have developed the quality of mental spaciousness, you feel that you can follow many ideas at once, that you cannot be overwhelmed, and that there is room inside your mind for everything that might demand your attention. You also feel that you can handle difficult situations, not necessarily because you already know the answers, but because you know you can create solutions as you need them.

When your mind is spacious, you are able to let go of your usual ways of organizing information. This letting go allows you to find solutions to problems that appear impossible. Many brain-teasers are designed to evoke this experience. For example: Try to make six straight rows of dots with exactly four dots in each row. This sounds simple until you try to do it using only twelve dots. A similar problem is to connect nine dots arranged in a three-by-three grid using only four straight lines, without lifting your pencil from the paper. Try working on these problems; as you discover a solution, you will have an experience of mental spaciousness. This experience of spaciousness will occur just before you solve the problem. It comes from surpassing the mental limitations that keep you from discovering a solution. This is why being told the answer to a problem does not have the same effect as finding the answer for yourself.

Spaciousness also helps you to create constructive outcomes from negative situations. If a coworker makes a mistake, expressing frustration is a natural response; however, it is rarely constructive. Spaciousness helps you to step back mentally from the immediate effects of the mistake. Then you can find ways to turn the mistake into a constructive, learning experience for you and your coworker.

Spaciousness can also help you at home. If your child tries to help you clean the dishes and drops a stack of them, making a mess on the floor, an automatic response can be annoyance. However, impulsively expressing your annoyance could easily lead to feelings of guilt; after all, your child is only trying to help. Spaciousness helps you to mentally step back, distancing yourself from the broken dishes at your feet. You can instantly take a broader perspective. You may remember similar mistakes you made when you were young. You also may imagine some years in the future when your child is grown, and realize that you both will be able to laugh over this. Your automatic response changes from annoyance to a calmer, "Oh, well." Instead of yelling and then feeling guilty, you end up chuckling inside.

Spaciousness helps you to let go of automatic ways of behaving and thinking, so that you can discover new and creative options. As you increase your spaciousness and balance it with the first four mental qualities, you will find that you are more imaginative. You will feel more humorous and more creative. Spaciousness is developed by opening techniques taught in chapter 5.

A PHILOSOPHICAL NOTE

Our mind uses the five mental qualities to create our experience of life. In Tibetan philosophy, each quality is associated with one of five elements. The elements symbolize mental processes, not mental objects. Each mental process is closely related to one mental quality. Spaciousness is associated with space, clarity is associated with air, warmth is associated with fire, pliancy is associated with water, and steadiness is associated with earth. In Tibetan Buddhist philosophy, the elements are arranged in a constructive and a destructive sequence. The constructive sequence is space, air, fire, water, and earth. The destructive sequence is earth, water, fire, air, and space. One particular manifestation of the destructive sequence occurs at death (this is described in texts such as *The Tibetan Book of the Dead*). However, the constructive and destructive sequences are going on in the mind constantly, and with extreme speed.

For example, imagine that you are faced with a situation that is entirely new to you, one in which you don't know how to respond. First, your mind uses the vastness of space to allow numerous possible reactions to form. Then, the clarity of air helps you to notice details of each of the possibilities, and distinguish between them. Next, fire and its warmth permit the mind to accept one or more of those possible responses into conscious awareness. The pliancy of water is then used to shift your mind from its stuck state of "I don't know what to do" to the possibilities you are now aware of. Finally, the steadiness of earth allows you to choose one particular response and express it. This demonstrates the constructive sequence of the five elements and their associated mental qualities.

If this first response were not appropriate, then you would need to return to space to generate a new potential response. To do that you would use the five qualities in the destructive sequence. The steadiness from earth that was allowing you to express your initial response would give way to the pliancy of water and the warmth of fire. This pliancy and warmth would allow you to disengage from continuing your response. Air and its associated clarity would help you to perceive the details that made the response inappropriate. Finally, all the mental energy that was involved in the response would be released into space and new possible responses would arise. This illustrates the destructive cycle of the five elements and mental qualities. Then the constructive process would begin again, allowing you to come up with a different response.

There are two important points to be made about the constructive and destructive cycles. First, the destructive cycle is not a bad thing. It is necessary, if we are to learn and change. Without the destructive cycle, we would not be able to change dysfunctional patterns. Second, spaciousness is a necessary step in both cycles. Spaciousness is often experienced as "I don't know." Unless we are willing to "not know," we cannot evoke either cycle fully. When one can fully and deliberately evoke either cycle, personal transformation becomes far more rapid.

There is no direct relationship between the five elements in Tibetan philosophy (earth, water, air, fire, and space) and the five elements in Taoist philosophy (earth, metal, water, wood, and fire). The Tibetan elements refer to processes of phenomena arising and dissolving. The Taoist elements refer to types of interactions between phenomena that are already present. The two schemes are referring to processes at completely different levels of existence. The Tibetan elements describe how phenomena arise (in Taoist terms, the process of going from *Wu-chi* to *Tai-chi*), and the Taoist elements describe how qualities of phenomena interact and perpetuate each other.

It is useful to look at an example of how the processes symbolized by the five Tibetan elements and their associated mental qualities function in a real-life situation.

A husband and wife have a minor disagreement one morning. The issue is not fully resolved before they both must leave for work. She returns home first, and is still thinking about their disagreement. Soon, her husband comes in through the door. He has had a hard day, traffic was bad on the way home, and he has a headache. Their minor disagreement from the morning is not on his mind at all.

As he enters the door, she notes that his brow is furrowed and sees it as a frown. She assumes this means that he is still angry with her from the morning's disagreement. However, we know that her assumption is incorrect.

Fortunately she is observant and does not jump to conclusions. She notices some minor details that contradict her assumption and realizes that his furrowed brow may have more to do with fatigue than anger. She asks him about his day and the drive home and discovers that her second interpretation was more accurate.

This situation of misperceiving and then correcting the misperception can happen in a fraction of a second. Yet both the destructive and constructive sequences of the five elements and their associated mental qualities are involved. The thoughts corresponding to each of the steps in both sequences are shown in the following table, along with the original and corrected perceptions.

HER ORIGINAL PERCEPTION: *He is frowning.*
HER CONCLUSION: *He is angry.*

	Element	Mental Quality	Thought
DESTRUCTIVE CYCLE	EARTH	Steadiness	*He is frowning and angry.*
	WATER	Pliancy	*His tone of voice and body language don't fit with anger.*
	FIRE	Warmth	*The differences are important; I need to pay attention to them.*
	AIR	Clarity	*His brow is furrowed, but his mouth and shoulders don't look tense. His voice doesn't sound angry.*
	SPACE	Spaciousness	*I don't know what he is feeling.*
CONSTRUCTIVE CYCLE	SPACE	Spaciousness	*I don't know what he is feeling.*
	AIR	Clarity	*His brow is furrowed. His lips are soft. His shoulders are slumped.*
	FIRE	Warmth	*He doesn't look angry, those other signs are meaningful.*
	WATER	Pliancy	*The furrowed brow, together with the soft lips and slumped shoulders mean something else; maybe he is tired or discouraged.*
	EARTH	Steadiness	*I'll focus on that assumption and ask about how his day went, and how he is feeling.*

HER NEW PERCEPTION: *He looks tired or discouraged.*
HER NEW CONCLUSION: *I should inquire about my perception that he is tired or discouraged.*

A DAY IN THE LIFE OF A MEDITATION TEACHER

We understand that we have just given you a lot of information, much of it new. The material on the five mental qualities, in particular, may be difficult to absorb. You may still be wondering how they relate to real-life situations. The following humorous story, told by Joe, illustrates how all five mental qualities came into play in a once-in-a-lifetime situation.

It was a bright sunny day in early September. I was sitting in the driver's seat of a moving truck with my five-year-old daughter, Tia, and her cat, Mitten, who was in a cardboard cat carrier. My wife, Marieke, and younger daughter, Kerani, had already left for our new house, about ninety miles away. The truck was fully loaded, and I started the engine. About ten seconds later, Mitten, terrified by the noise of the large diesel engine, clawed his way out of the cat carrier. Since Marieke had already left, there was nothing else to do but try to calm Mitten and drive onward. Mitten seemed to respond to Tia's soothing, and she was able to place him back in the cat carrier. Twenty minutes later, we were driving at high speed in heavy freeway traffic with Mitten sitting calmly, we thought, in the now-open cat carrier. Suddenly, everything changed. With a yowl of fright, Mitten leaped out of the cat carrier onto the seat of the van as a stream of diarrhea erupted from his back end.

At this point, I needed all my mental qualities. Steadiness helped me to stay aware of traffic so that I could keep the truck on the road, in spite of the distractions inside the cab. Pliancy helped me to switch my attention back and forth rapidly between the road and the cab. Warmth helped me to accept the unsavory fact that the best place for Mitten, mess and all, was next to me so that he would feel calm enough to stop emptying his intestines. Clarity helped me to sort through a number of options very quickly and arrive at a decision. Spaciousness helped me to keep from being overwhelmed so that I could stay calm and think creatively; this also helped keep my daughter from being frightened or upset.

These mental qualities guided my actions automatically. I immediately grabbed Mitten by the scruff of the neck and pulled him next to me on the seat, thus stopping his panic reaction. I then guided the truck over to the next off ramp, remembering that I had thrown some old blankets and towels in the back where I could get to them easily. Once off the freeway, we found a place to stop. I found the old towels and cleaned up Mitten and enough of the mess to make the rest of the trip bearable. We started off again, with Mitten under the seat, where he made no more outbursts. As we traveled, spaciousness helped me and my daughter to see how absolutely funny the whole situation was. Neither of us got upset, and we were able to laugh at it easily.

The meditative practices we describe in part I are designed to develop your mental qualities in a balanced manner. You will strengthen your five mental qualities during your practice. As you develop these qualities, your reactions to life events will become more constructive and creative. These creative, spontaneous reactions will occur during routine events in your daily life, as well as during the unusual and more difficult situations that you encounter from time to time.

We end this chapter with Brian and Maria's reactions to their introductory meditation class, and a note about goals.

Brian's Reflections upon the Introductory Session

Brian and Maria both attended an introductory meditation session. Though they had different experiences of the class and different goals for meditation, each was enthusiastic about learning.

On his way home from the introductory session, Brian reflects on his experience. One of the nice surprises had been that the other people in the room all looked normal. Some were in sweats, some were in work clothes. There were even a few in business suits. "Hmm, this can't be all that weird," he had thought.

Brian found the idea of the five mental qualities interesting. As he thinks about these now, he can see examples of how they work in his life. He finds it quite easy to focus on things, and correctly decides that he has a good deal of steadiness. He also is good at analyzing and picking out details. This comes from his mental clarity. However, he remembers numerous times when he was unable to change his focus or the way he was doing things. He has a reputation for being "stubborn" or "pigheaded." He also realizes that while he analyzes well, he has difficulty understanding others' perspectives. This has led to accusations that he is "closed-minded." He now realizes that those difficulties come from a lack of pliancy and warmth. He admires his ability to focus and analyze, and realizes that he does not need to lose those. He simply needs to develop the complementary qualities, pliancy and warmth.

Spaciousness intrigues Brian and he recalls isolated instances when he had flashes of inspiration. He feels that he could use a lot more spaciousness. He had asked the teacher if he should practice only the techniques that developed the qualities he thought he needed: pliancy, warmth, and spaciousness. *That is a good question*, the teacher had responded, *people need all the mental qualities, and they must be balanced. Practice all the meditation techniques in the proper sequence so that you will develop all the qualities in a balanced manner. You will find that you need to practice some techniques more than others, depending on the mental qualities you need to develop most.*

One of the things that Brian liked about the session was the emphasis on practical results. During one part of the session, the attendees were asked to think about what they would like meditation to help them achieve, their goals or intended results from meditating. They were asked to write down one or two goals in each of four life areas: health, performance, relationships, and spirituality. The teacher said that if they had questions about possible goals, they could speak to him during the break.

Brian's health goals were easy for him to pick. He knew about his health issues that were stress related, and it seemed that meditation could help with those. He decided that his health goals would be to reduce his neck tension and maybe even lower his blood pressure.

Brian hadn't been able to think of a performance goal at first. The ones that came to mind seemed too big for him to have any hope of accomplishing. After some reflection he decided to work on improving his golf game. He asked the teacher about this, because it seemed a little odd to use meditation for that goal. His teacher had smiled and said, *Meditation doesn't have to be completely serious. It is OK to use it for lighter things. Applying meditation to your golf game will help you improve, and make it more relaxing for you. You will also see improvement quickly and that will demonstrate the effectiveness of the techniques to you.*

Brian chose as his relationship goal to reduce the frequency and intensity of his angry outbursts, both at work and at home, and especially with his children. While he is not violent, he does have a short temper and often says things that he wishes he hadn't. Brian was concerned that meditation would just make him ignore the situations that upset him. This would not be good, because he does have to deal with those situations. He had expressed this worry to his teacher, who responded, *Many people think meditation is about being calm and distant. That is incorrect. It is about being calm and present. You practice the basic techniques in solitude to train your mind to perform better at everything else you do. You are more effective at living.*

Brian was somewhat confused about the spirituality goal, as he does not consider himself religious. When he asked his teacher about it he was told, *Being spiritual can be different than being religious. What do you want to live for that is bigger than you are, that seems holy or sacred?* Brian identified a sense of being at peace with people and the world as something spiritual. *Fine; cultivating a deeper and deeper sense of peace is certainly a spiritual goal, and one that will benefit others as well as yourself.*

Brian feels pleased with the goals he has chosen. A part of his mind seems very satisfied and happy, as though a door were opening in a wall that has been enclosing him. To be sure, meditation does not look like a quick or magical fix. But in some way that makes it seem even more real.

Maria's Reflections upon the Introductory Session

As Maria returns home from the introductory meditation class, she reflects on the experience before calling her friend, Susan, to tell her how it went. She realizes that it was not as strange or unusual as she had been afraid it would be. The other attendees seemed to be rather average people in usual clothing. The teacher was dressed casually and looked no more mysterious than someone she might see in the produce section of the supermarket. She saw no sign that anyone was going to make her follow a different religion. In fact, the teacher was quite accepting of her goals, and none of them had anything to do with a different religion.

Maria feels a little more able to accept herself after hearing the presentation on the five mental qualities. She knows that she finds it easy to go from one thing to another—having to change plans does not cause her any difficulties. However, she often has difficulty staying on a particular course of action. She frequently changes plans even when she doesn't have to, sometimes to the frustration of those around her. People have called her "flaky," but she resents that because she likes her ability to change easily. As she reflects on this, she concludes that her ability to change easily is related to mental pliancy, and her pliancy needs to be balanced by more steadiness.

Maria also notes how she is very open to new ideas or multiple ways of looking at a situation. However, she often jumps to a new idea before analyzing the previous one. This has led to accusations that she is "superficial." She realizes that this occurs because her natural warmth was not balanced by enough clarity.

Maria had just assumed that these problems were part of her personality and would be with her forever. "That's just me," she used to say. Now she has the sense that she will be able to change. It is not that she is "flaky" or "superficial"; those traits actually come from the presence of two valuable mental qualities, pliancy and warmth. She simply needs to balance those qualities with steadiness and clarity.

Maria also likes the idea of having goals for her meditation practice. Her health goal was easy for her to pick. She wants to reduce the frequency and intensity of her headaches. They are bothersome, and while the medicine she takes for them helps reduce the discomfort, she does not like the way the pills make her feel. The teacher said, *Meditation often helps reduce the frequency and intensity of headaches. You may even find that you are able to stop a headache before it starts. However, headaches, or any physical symptom, can be a warning sign from the body. So you need to work with your physician and let her know if the headaches do not improve.* Maria agreed to continue to see her doctor and to use the meditation as a complementary form of treatment.

Her performance goal is to give better presentations at work. She tends to get nervous and easily flustered when speaking in front of other people, and would like to be more at ease. Her difficulty in giving presentations is keeping her from moving ahead in her company. She was a little worried about using meditation to help her improve at something that is so connected with personal gain. When she brought this up with the teacher, he said, *That is a good question. We do not want to use meditation to pursue mere monetary gain. However, in this case, you are working on improving your ability to communicate. That will help you and your company. The advancement will be secondary to that, and is not your primary goal. So using meditation to improve your ability to make presentations is a good goal.*

Maria's relationship goal is to be more patient and less nagging at home. When something upsets her, she tends to complain about it more than is helpful. She knows she complains too much at times, but she can't seem to stop herself. Maria would like to be able to let go of things that are not important, and to express her dissatisfaction about the things that matter in ways that get results.

Maria knew that her spirituality goal had to be related to her Christian faith. Her spiritual goal is to have a deeper relationship with God. She was a little concerned that meditation would not fit with that goal, that it was too Eastern to be used by a Christian.

The teacher told her, *Christianity has a long tradition of using meditation for strengthening the personal relationship with God. You will certainly be able to use the meditation exercises you practice to become a better Christian.* Realizing that the teacher was very comfortable with her goal of developing a deeper connection with God helped Maria feel more accepting of this.

WHAT DO I WANT TO GET OUT OF THIS?

Now give some thought to goals that you might have. Since you are going to spend time meditating, what would you like it to help you with? Think about the four areas of your life: health, performance, relationships, and spirituality. Decide on one or two positive changes in each of those areas and write them down. You do not need to know exactly what you want. It is all right to change your goals as you proceed through the book. Some suggestions in each of the areas follow.

HEALTH—reducing stress, decreasing muscle tension, improving general health, making positive lifestyle changes

PERFORMANCE—improving at a sport or other recreational activity, doing better at a particular task, being able to complete a task faster or with less effort, being able to perform a task that is currently beyond you, learning a new skill

RELATIONSHIPS—decreasing anger, increasing patience, increasing understanding, being more gentle with others, being firmer at setting boundaries

SPIRITUALITY—increasing one's understanding of one's current religion, increasing an awareness of connection with others, increasing a sense of peace, becoming more loving

two

centering: steadying your mind

•

Anchor the wild elephant of the mind
To the steadfast pillar of the object of meditation

The Essence of the Middle Way

•

Centering is the most basic meditation practice, and it is the foundation for all further meditative work. It is what most people think of when they hear the word "meditation." Although centering is basic, it is also critical because it develops the mental quality of steadiness. Without sufficient mental steadiness, you will not be able to practice more advanced techniques. Fortunately, centering develops steadiness quickly, and most people can move on after two to three weeks.

To practice centering, pick something to focus your awareness on. This is called your center. Then focus your awareness on your center, and return your awareness to your center when you get distracted. While focusing on your center, you are to stay aware of your environment. Centering trains your mind to be calm and focused.

Centering consists of two activities:

- Focus your awareness on your center, while staying aware of your environment;

- If you get distracted and lose track of your center, bring your awareness back to it.

It is possible to center on any of a number of things. Centering on different things can have different effects. The most common centering technique is to focus on the sensations in the lower abdomen as you breathe. There are several reasons for this: First, and most practically, those sensations are always present. Since your breath is always with you, you can practice this basic technique anywhere. Second, centering on the lower abdomen tends to be relaxing. Third, it tends to promote a smooth, easy breathing pattern, which facilitates the development of a calm, focused mental state.

Centering, however, is neither a relaxation exercise nor a breathing exercise. It is a focusing exercise that is a foundation for further meditative work. Let's follow Brian and Maria through their experiences with centering.

BRIAN'S FIRST MEDITATION SESSION

It is 6:10 A.M., and Brian has just awakened for his first meditation practice session. He has decided to practice meditation for fifteen minutes each morning. He figures that he will practice six days a week, and that will give him the ninety minutes per week that his teacher advised as a minimum. Getting up about fifteen or twenty minutes earlier than usual did not seem so difficult when he was thinking about it last night. Now he is not so sure. He feels a little stiff, and he is tempted to crawl back into his nice warm bed. He shrugs off the temptation and pulls on a warm pair of sweat pants and a sweatshirt. Still feeling groggy, he washes his face in cold water. Somewhat awakened, he goes into the living room and, placing a pillow from the couch on the floor next to the wall, he sits down on it cross-legged.

Brian remembers that he is to start each session by thinking about his goals for meditation. *Focus your intention at the beginning of each session,* his teacher said. *That will increase your motivation and help you to make faster progress.*

"Good question," Brian thinks. "What am I up this early for, anyway?"

Brian reviews his long-range goals mentally: reducing his neck tension and blood pressure, improving his golf game, controlling his temper, and developing a sense of being at peace with others. He also remembers the immediate goal of this session: learning to focus his mind and maintain awareness of the sensations in his lower abdomen. Remembering these goals takes only a few seconds and completes the intention phase of the session. Brian then begins the execution phase.

He places his palms on his lower abdomen so his thumbs are over his navel. He centers his awareness on the sensations in his abdomen under his palms. At first he feels nothing, and then he notices a little motion as he breathes in and out. He catches himself trying to change his breathing and make it deeper. He remembers the instructions, *It's not a breathing exercise, it's a centering exercise. How fast, slow, shallow, or deep you breathe does not matter. Just be aware of the sensations.* Brian continues to notice the sensations of movement in his lower abdomen, and then begins to feel a sense of warmth there. After a couple of minutes he finds himself thinking about work. He tries to force these thoughts out of his mind, however the thoughts seem to get louder. He is beginning to get frustrated when he remembers his teacher saying, *It's OK to have other thoughts, so don't try to get rid of them; just tell them, "later," and focus your awareness on your lower abdomen again.* Brian smiles. He begins to think, "later," as the thoughts about work arise.

The thoughts subside, and he feels the comfortable warmth in his lower abdomen more clearly. After another couple of minutes, Brian notices that there is some tension in his neck. It is not getting worse, but it is certainly not going away. Immediately the thoughts start in again: "You're not relaxing, you're not doing it right, you might as well stop now! You'll never get this. You're wasting your time." His breathing speeds up a bit and he tenses in response to these thoughts. Again his teacher's words come to mind. *It's NOT a relaxation exercise, it's a mental exercise, a centering technique. You are training your mind. If you relax, great. If not, then you are still training your mind and that is what counts.* As Brian remembers this, he is able to stop trying to relax. He returns his awareness to his lower abdomen. His tension stops building and eases. He settles down and feels more comfortable. After another couple of minutes, Brian hears the alarm on his watch go off, indicating that it is time to stop the session. He is surprised that fifteen minutes have gone by already.

Before finishing the session, Brian reflects on his experience. He notes how much noise his mind made. He remembers how hard it was to stay centered on the sensations, and starts to criticize his performance. He then remembers his teacher saying, *It is normal to have some difficulty at first. You are doing well if you keep bringing your attention back to the sensations in your lower abdomen.* Brian decides that while he did get distracted, he did pretty well at bringing his awareness back to his lower abdomen. After these reflections on his experience, Brian brings his awareness to his whole body, he remembers the day, the time, and his surroundings, and then wiggles his fingers and toes a bit before he gets up to continue the rest of his day.

MARIA'S FIRST MEDITATION SESSION

Maria is getting ready for her first meditation session after her day at work. She has convinced her husband to watch the children during her meditation sessions, three days a week. This will give her thirty minutes to practice on each of those days. He had balked a little at this, but assented when she told him it was to help her have more patience and fewer headaches. She changes out of her work clothes into less constricting garb, then goes out into the garage with a blanket and gets into the front seat of her car. She feels a little silly doing this, but it is really the only place where she knows that she will not be disturbed. Sitting down in the front passenger seat, she adjusts it so that she is comfortable, then places the blanket over herself so that she feels warm.

As she starts the session, she remembers her teacher's words. *Focus your intention as you begin each session by remembering your immediate and long-range goals. Answer the question, "Why am I spending my time doing this?" That will facilitate your practice.* Maria thinks about her goals for a minute: relief from her headaches, less anxiety giving presentations, more patience at home, and a deeper relationship with God. She also remembers her immediate goal for the session: keeping her mind focused on her lower abdomen and going back to it if distracted. After remembering her goals, Maria begins the execution phase of the session.

She adjusts her position in the seat and places her hands in her lap. She centers her awareness on the sensations she is feeling in her lower abdomen. At first, she can't feel anything, so she arranges her hands on her abdomen with her thumbs over her navel. This places her palms and fingers over her lower abdomen and she is able to feel things more clearly there.

Almost immediately she is hit by an urge to shift position. She tries to remain still, but she becomes more and more uncomfortable. She doesn't understand how she can meditate if she can't even sit still for a few minutes. She remembers a comment from her teacher: *Meditation doesn't mean sitting still in unnatural positions, especially in the beginning. If you are feeling uncomfortable, shift position. If you have to move every couple of minutes, that is fine, just shift position and then go back to what you are supposed to be practicing*. Maria allows her shoulders to wiggle, and moves her legs back and forth. After doing this a few times, her need to shift decreases and her body seems to settle into position.

The first sensations Maria notices are a slight expansion and contraction in her abdomen as she breathes. She feels a little self-conscious about this but remembers, *Even though the air goes in and out of your lungs, your body has to make room for the air to come in. That means that your abdomen will expand a bit as you breathe in and will contract a bit as you breathe out*. The expansion and contraction feels gentle and peaceful, and Maria smiles to herself.

As she continues to focus on her abdomen, Maria notices some warmth in her hands and then in the skin of her abdomen under her hands. At first, the sensations are faint and she finds herself distracted numerous times. The distractions are so numerous, she wonders if she is doing the technique correctly. *The key to centering is not how long you stay focused, but how easy it is for you to go back to your center.* As Maria continues to recall her attention to the sensations in her lower abdomen, she finds the sense of warmth under her hands growing. Soon she begins to feel a pleasant sensation of warmth all through her lower abdomen. Her mind begins to drift off and suddenly she jumps, realizing that she was almost asleep. She opens her eyes and looks at her watch and is surprised to notice that twenty minutes have gone by. She remembers the instructions, *Make sure you stay awake during the exercise. Sleeping is not the same as meditating*. She adjusts her position in the seat, closes her eyes and goes back to being aware of the sensations in her lower abdomen. Her mind refocuses itself, and a short time later she hears her watch alarm go off.

As Maria hears the alarm, she reflects on her experience. She remembers that a lot of the distractions were thoughts from the day at work. She notes how calming it felt to ignore those thoughts and return her focus to her lower abdomen. She remembers how she almost fell asleep, and resolves to wash her face in cold water before the next session to make sure she stays awake. After these reflections, Maria brings her awareness to her whole body, reorients to time and place, wiggles her fingers and toes a bit, and then opens her eyes, feeling refreshed and calm.

THE BASICS OF CENTERING

Centering is the practice of maintaining continuous awareness of something, while staying awake and aware of the environment. The *center* is what you maintain awareness of. Brian and Maria were both practicing a centering technique in which the center was the sensations in the lower abdomen.

Centering develops the mental quality of steadiness. Steadiness helps your mind stay focused more easily. When your mind is centered it is like a boat at anchor. The boat does not stay exactly still; it drifts back and forth. However, after it drifts a little bit, the anchor chain tightens and brings it back over the anchor point. In the same way, it is natural for your awareness to drift somewhat during centering. As long as you keep bringing your awareness back to your center, you are doing the practice correctly.

INSTRUCTIONS FOR EXTENDED CENTERING PRACTICE

1. Sit in a comfortable position, in a place where you are not likely to be disturbed.
2. Focus your intention, by thinking about your long-range goals for meditation and your immediate goal for the session. (Your immediate goal for this extended centering technique is to maintain awareness of the sensations in your lower abdomen.)
3. Notice the sensations in your lower abdomen (below your navel). If you have difficulty sensing this area, place your hands on your abdomen with your thumbs on top of your navel and your palms facing you. In this position, your palms and fingers will rest on your lower abdomen. Note that the lower abdomen includes the area to the sides, and not just the front of the body.
4. Breathe comfortably; there is no need to try to change your breathing pattern. Note that your breathing may vary naturally during the exercise.
5. You should still notice other things going on around you. Don't get so absorbed by your center that you lose track of your environment.
6. If you do get distracted, simply bring your awareness back to your center, the sensations in your lower abdomen. If you find yourself thinking about things, just tell the thoughts, "later."
7. It is all right to get distracted. The important thing is to learn to come back to your center.

Once you can maintain your focus on the sensations in your lower abdomen for about thirty seconds without getting distracted and without straining, you are ready to move on. Depending on how much you practice and your natural ability, this usually takes from one to three weeks.

Remember, centering on the lower abdomen is just a beginning. As you learn other meditative techniques and applications, you will learn to center on other things. Centering on different things leads to different experiences.

BRIEF CENTERING PRACTICE

The centering technique described above is to be done in extended practice sessions. You should practice the extended technique for a minimum of fifteen minutes each time. By practicing this technique you will improve at centering, and your mind will become steadier. But if you practice only the extended technique, you will inadvertently teach your mind two things. First, that your mind will always have fifteen or more minutes to get centered. It will not learn to center quickly. Second, that centering is something that you do in the setting where you practice meditation, and nowhere else. Your mind will not learn to center in other places. So, if you only practice the extended technique, you will severely limit your progress, and your ability to use the resulting steadiness.

The solution to this dilemma is to practice a brief centering technique several times throughout the day. The brief sessions should last no more than a minute. You should do at least five brief sessions per day and they should be done in a variety of settings. Then your mind will learn to center quickly, anywhere, and anytime you need it to.

A useful brief centering practice is to center on a simple thought pattern for about thirty seconds. One of the most helpful patterns that we have found is the sequence "calm—relaxed." This allows the brief centering practice to double as a stress-reduction exercise. You can try other thought patterns as well. Centering on different thoughts will yield different results.

Brian's Experience with Brief Centering Practice

Brian is sitting at his desk on a Tuesday morning, preparing for a meeting. He is a little stressed about getting all his notes together. He suddenly hears his watch beep twice and realizes that an hour has gone by since he arrived. He first thinks "I don't have time for this," and then remembers his teacher's words, *Brief practice is critically important if you want to really benefit from meditation. Also, taking a few seconds from your work will actually improve your efficiency.* Brian leans back in his chair and focuses his intention by remembering his goals for meditation. He also remembers his goal for this technique, to center on a thought pattern for a few seconds. He then closes his eyes and takes a deep breath as he thinks the word "calm." He then releases the air as he thinks the word "relaxed." He then breathes naturally, thinking "calm" as he breathes in and "relaxed" as he breathes out. After four or five breaths he reflects on the experience. He decides he does feel a little bit calmer and has a little less tension in his shoulders. However, the effect of the exercise is slight and he wonders if he is really succeeding at this. Brian remembers, *The results from brief practice are quite variable, especially in the beginning. Simply do the technique for a few seconds and accept the results, whatever they are.* Brian opens his eyes and goes back to working on preparing for his meeting. The whole practice session took less than a minute.

A hour later Brian's watch beeps again. He is still quite busy preparing for the meeting. He has promised himself that he will do the brief technique at least five times per day. He decides that he will skip this time and practice it in one hour, just before his meeting.

That afternoon, Brian hears his watch beep again. He is feeling all right about how the meeting went earlier, and feels happy about doing the brief technique. He closes his eyes, focuses his intention, and takes a deep breath as he thinks "calm" and then releases the air as he thinks "relaxed." He then breathes naturally as he thinks "calm" on the inhalation and "relaxed" on the exhalation. After a couple of breaths he is starting to feel calm and peaceful. He feels like continuing the practice because it feels so nice. However, he remembers, *When doing brief practice you must stop after a few seconds. Do not continue the exercise for more than a minute at most. If you do you will lose the effect of training your mind to respond rapidly.* Brian reluctantly decides to stop. He reflects on the experience and then opens his eyes.

As Brian finishes his ride home from work, he pulls into his garage and turns off his car. He is about ready to head inside when he realizes that this is a perfect time to do the brief centering. As soon as he realizes that, he notices how tired he feels and how much eyestrain he is experiencing. He settles back into the seat, closes his eyes and focuses his intention to center on a thought pattern for about a minute. He takes a deep breath as he thinks "calm" and releases the air as he thinks "relaxed." He continues to think "calm" and "relaxed" as he breathes easily. After several breaths he feels lighter, like he has released a load off of his shoulders. His neck feels looser, and his eyes are not as tired. He reflects on the experience and then goes inside, feeling more relaxed then he usually does when he arrives home.

Maria's Experience with Brief Centering Practice

Maria is sitting at her desk at work. She has just hung up the phone, and glances at a card she has taped near the far left corner of the desk. It reads, "calm—alert." She remembers her commitment to do brief practice at least six times per day. Things are quiet right now, so she decides to practice. She sits up and focuses on her intention by remembering her goals for meditation. She also remembers her goal for this technique, to center on a thought pattern. Maria then keeps her eyes open as she takes a deep breath, thinking "calm" as she does so. She then breathes out, thinking "alert." Maria then breathes naturally, thinking "calm" as she breathes in and "alert" as she breathes out. After several breaths, she reflects on her experience. She notices that her head feels somewhat clearer and she feels less sleepy.

Later that morning Maria is walking down the hall to her supervisor's office. She suddenly remembers the card on her desk and wonders if she could practice while walking. She remembers, *Meditation is not just to be practiced sitting down with your eyes closed. The brief techniques especially are designed to be practiced in many situations. You should try them and find ways to do them throughout the day. Just be careful about doing them when you are supposed to be concentrating on something else, like when you are driving*. Maria decides that now is as good a time as any to do the brief technique. So, while walking, she focuses on her intention. She then just starts thinking "calm" as she breathes in and "alert" as she breathes out. After several breaths she stops and reflects on her experience. She feels a little different but is not sure just how. She then realizes that she is not quite as tense as she usually is when going to meet her supervisor.

After lunch, Maria is at a meeting and finds her attention starting to wane. She wishes that she were more alert and remembers her brief centering technique. She straightens her back a bit and focuses on her intention to center on a thought pattern for a few seconds. She then thinks "calm" as she breathes in and "alert" as she breathes out. After a couple of breaths, she feels more energized and the room seems to appear in sharper focus. She finds that she is able to pay attention to the presentation more easily.

That evening, Maria is getting her children ready for bed. They are tired, irritable, and quarreling. As she listens to them tease each other, she feels her patience wearing thin. Before she scolds them she decides to use the brief centering exercise. She takes a deep breath and thinks "calm," and then releases it as she thinks "steady." She closes her eyes for a few breaths as she continues to center on the thoughts "calm" and "steady." Her irritation recedes, and she feels like she has a stronger connection with the earth, more grounded. She reflects that it is normal for tired children to quarrel, and so she does not need to stop their minor squabbling, but can focus on the solution, which is getting them into bed.

INSTRUCTIONS FOR BRIEF CENTERING PRACTICE

As you can see, the brief centering technique should be used in many different situations. It should also be kept brief. Even if you do not feel any effect from the technique, you must stop after a minute. The brevity of the technique teaches your mind to center quickly. By practicing in a variety of situations, you learn to use centering anywhere.

The instructions for the brief centering technique follow.

1. Focus your intention by thinking about what you are to do: You are going to center on a simple thought pattern for about a minute. Focusing your intention should take only a second.
2. Take a deep breath as you think the word "calm." Release the breath as you think "relaxed." Then breathe freely and continue to think "calm" as you inhale, and "relaxed" as you exhale.
3. After about a minute (about ten breaths), reflect on the result.

TIPS

You can do the technique with your eyes closed or open.

You can use other words to center on. We recommend that at first you use combinations such as the ones Brian and Maria used: "calm—relaxed," "calm— alert," "calm—steady."

Be creative about finding times to fit the brief technique into your day. Common times to practice are before and after meals, before or after driving somewhere (not while driving), before switching tasks, while doing routine tasks such as household chores, in the bathroom (instead of reading a magazine). You can also use an alarm or other environmental signal to prompt you.

Practicing the brief centering technique at least five times per day will develop your ability to center quickly, which will enable you to experience the benefits of mental steadiness throughout the day. Remember, the brief technique is just as important as the extended technique.

Brian's Results from Centering

Brian is waking up for his morning centering session. He has been practicing for two weeks, and finds it easier to get up now. He washes his face with cold water to get fully awake, goes into the living room, and sits down on the cushion against the wall.

Brian closes his eyes and focuses his intention by thinking briefly about his goals for meditation. He also thinks about his goal for this session, centering on the sensations in his lower abdomen. He places his hands on his abdomen and focuses his awareness there. As is usual for him now, he notices the gentle movement of his abdomen as he breathes. Then he feels the sense of comfortable warmth there. Some thoughts come in about what he needs to do later in the day, but he is able to maintain his awareness of his lower abdomen. He feels a sense of comfort in his arms and shoulders. He gets distracted briefly by some thoughts about his car, an errand he needs to do, and a meeting at work. But, after each distraction, he is able to refocus his awareness on the sensations in his lower abdomen.

Brian's mind feels quiet and peaceful. He is aware of a pleasant warmth in his lower abdomen, and of a gentle sense of expansion and contraction as he inhales and exhales. He feels like a mountain—solid, steady, and connected with the earth. His face has a soft smile on it. The practice feels relaxed and natural. Again, he is surprised when his watch alarm beeps to signal the end of the session. He reflects on how comfortable the practice is for him and how easily he can refocus after getting distracted. He also thinks about how this practice has helped him start the day in a much calmer state of mind. He then returns his awareness to his whole body, reorients to time and place, and stretches as he opens his eyes.

Later that day, Brian leans back in his chair at work, closes his eyes and notices his breathing. He focuses his intention to center on the thought pattern "calm—relaxed." He thinks "calm" as he breathes in, and "relaxed" as he breathes out. He allows other thoughts to go on, as long as one of the thoughts he has as he breathes in is "calm" and one of the thoughts he has as he breathes out is "relaxed." He allows his breathing rate to be natural and does not alter it or try to breathe deeply. He finds that after a burst of noisy thoughts, his mind gets quieter and his neck and shoulder muscles relax. After ten or so breaths, he reflects on his experience. He notices how the exercise sometimes evokes a definite sense of relaxation, but other times seems to have little or no effect. He realizes that the positive effects have become more frequent as he has kept practicing over the past couple of weeks.

One night, Brian is having some difficulty falling asleep. He feels tired but can't seem to settle down. He decides to try using the centering technique to help himself get to sleep. He lies on his back and places his hands on his lower abdomen. He then focuses on the sensations there as he thinks "calm" and "relaxed" over and over. After a few minutes, Brian feels his body loosen and his mind becoming more peaceful. A couple of minutes more and he feels warm and relaxed and his mind starts to drift. He rolls on his side, pulls the covers around himself, and falls asleep.

Brian asked his teacher if this was all right. His teacher responded, *You can certainly apply centering to help you get to sleep. Meditation is meant to be used. You combined elements from the extended technique and the brief technique to suit your needs. And, it worked. Good job!*

After two weeks of practice, Brian is pleased with his progress. He enjoys the extended practice. It is a good way to start the day. The brief practice is particularly useful for him. He finds that doing it frequently keeps his stress level down throughout the day. If he forgets to do it on a particular day, he notices a definite increase in tension. When he does use the brief technique, not only is his stress level lower, but he is also able to shrug off minor annoyances. He gets less upset while driving and is more relaxed around the house. Using the centering technique to get to sleep is an added bonus. Brian is looking forward to the next practice—attending.

Maria's Results from Centering

Maria is sitting in her car, preparing to do the extended centering exercise. She has been practicing for about two weeks and feels less self-conscious about it. It is becoming more of a routine. She adjusts the blanket over herself, places her palms on her lower abdomen, and closes her eyes. She thinks briefly about her goals for meditation, and then focuses her awareness on the sensations in her lower abdomen.

After a few seconds, she finds herself thinking about her day at work and realizes that she has lost track of the sensations in her abdomen. She refocuses her awareness on the sensations of movement there. Then she gets distracted by an itch on her leg. She scratches it and refocuses on her lower abdomen. She continues to get distracted every few seconds for several more minutes, but after each distraction, she simply refocuses her awareness on her lower abdomen.

Gradually she begins to feel a sense of comfortable warmth in her palms. As the sense of warmth in her palms spreads into her abdomen, the distractions become less frequent. However, she still gets distracted at least every minute. Sometimes the distractions are sensations, but most of the time they are thoughts about the house, her husband, her children, or work. She wonders if she is doing the technique correctly, and remembers, *Many people find they get distracted frequently during centering practice. The purpose of centering is to develop enough mental steadiness so that you can do the more advanced meditative practices. Once you can maintain your awareness of your center for twenty to thirty seconds, and you can refocus you awareness easily when distracted, you are doing well enough.*

Maria realizes that recalling her teacher's words is another distraction, but it relieves her performance anxiety and she is able to refocus on the sensations in her lower abdomen. When her timer goes off, Maria reflects on her experience. The exercise is calming, but not as settling as she thought meditation was supposed to be. She worries that if she has this much difficulty with the first practice, then she will find the more advanced practices impossible. She had complained about this to her teacher, who responded, *If your mind is jumping around during the centering sessions it may be because it has a lot of natural pliancy. If that is so, you will find the next practice—attending—to be a lot easier then centering. Just because a practice comes later in the sequence does not mean that it will be more difficult.* Maria accepts the fact that her mind likes to jump around. She is able to maintain awareness of the sensations in her abdomen for thirty seconds at a time. She is therefore ready to move on to the next practice, attending.

The next day, Maria pushes back from her chair at work and looks out the window. She focuses her intention to center on the thought pattern "calm—alert." She wants to be able to remain calm while also keeping her eyes open and staying aware of her surroundings. She thinks the word "calm" as she inhales, and thinks the word "alert" as she exhales. She notices that her breathing seems to deepen a bit and she sits up a little straighter in her chair. After a few more breaths, she feels as if her vision is sharper and more focused. She also feels a sense of strength in her body, as if her muscles are toned and ready for action. After about a minute, she stops centering and reflects on her experience. She notices how the sense of being calm and alert is different from her usual state during the day. She also senses how it is getting easier to focus her mind.

As Maria reflects on her meditation practice thus far, she has mixed feelings. She finds the extended practice helpful because she can let go of the events from work before being with her family. This improves her interactions at home. However, the extended sessions are not quite as restful as she had hoped they would be. On the other hand, the brief practice is especially useful for her. When she is starting to feel like too many things are demanding her attention at once, the brief practice helps her stay calm and keep from getting scattered. She can use the technique anywhere, walking down the hall, before and after driving, even during conversations. Sometimes she finds herself thinking "calm—alert" spontaneously, even before she realizes she is getting upset. This is a positive change in her life and she is hoping the next practice, attending, will be just as useful.

CONCLUSION

Centering requires you to keep your mind focused on something. What you focus on is what we call your "center." You can center on a variety of physical or mental objects. The basic techniques described in this chapter involve centering on the sensations in your lower abdomen, and centering on a simple thought pattern.

While you are centering, you should maintain continuous awareness of your center while remaining aware of the environment. As long as you are staying aware of your center, you are still centered, even if you are noticing other things. If you lose awareness of your center, simply bring your awareness back to it.

Centering is to be done in extended sessions of at least fifteen minutes for a total time of at least ninety minutes per week. It is also to be done in brief periods of up to one minute several times per day.

Once you can center for thirty seconds without being distracted, then you are ready to move on to the next practice—attending. This usually takes just one to three weeks of practice, especially if you practice both the extended and brief exercises.

Remember: the brief practice sessions are just as important as the extended practice sessions. In fact, as Maria experienced, you may get more noticeable benefits from the brief sessions than you do from the extended sessions. So practice both, because one reinforces the other.

TIPS

Remember to focus your intention at the start of each session by reviewing your goals for meditation. This takes only a couple of seconds.

Comfort is important. Make sure that you are warm and that you are sitting comfortably. If you want to move or shift position during the session, that is fine. For example, if you have a cold and need to blow your nose during the session, just do it and then return to meditating.

Stay awake during the sessions. It can help to wash your face in cold water at the beginning of the session.

The brief practice is extremely important. You can do it before and after meals, after driving, on the bus, while using the bathroom or taking a shower, before starting a task, after finishing a task, and other similar times throughout the day.

You can also use centering to fall asleep at bedtime. Simply center on your lower abdomen while thinking "calm—relaxed" after you lie down in bed. It is all right to use centering for this purpose. It is a simple and effective application of meditation.

three

Attending: Building a Mind That is Flexible and Tolerant

You might have attained such incredible mindfulness that nothing can distract you, but it is of little value if you have not developed a warm heart.

The Kadampas

Now that you have developed some steadiness, it is time to move on, and improve your mental pliancy and warmth. The practice for developing those qualities is called "attending." Attending is an efficient practice, because it develops two mental qualities at once. As you practice attending, your mind will move more quickly and you will be able to keep track of more things at once. You will become more open and aware of what is going on around and inside you.

To practice attending, you center on something and then pay attention to what else is going on. When something distracts you, you identify it as precisely as possible. Then you disengage from the distraction and move your awareness back to your center. We use the word "disengage" instead of "let go" because many times you need to exert some effort to get away from what is distracting you. If the distraction has grabbed you, passively letting go will not help you. You must exert some effort and disengage from the distraction that has caught your attention.

When you are practicing attending, you are like someone sitting on the bank of a river watching things go by. You notice the things that pass, but you do not get in the river to check them out. Occasionally, something going by catches you and you have to disengage from it to keep from being pulled in. Once you have disengaged, you just go back to watching.

Attending can be described most generally as being aware of the "now." However, the "now" is quite complex. Is the "now" the memories that you are having, the sensations that you are experiencing, the thoughts that you are thinking, or the emotions that you are feeling? If you reflect on the scenes that you see in the nightly news, your "now" will be different than if you reflect on the kind things that people do for each other. Attending techniques help you to understand how your mind chooses which "now" to experience. Eventually, you will be able to influence that choice, and experience a "now" that is peaceful.

When you start attending, you pay most attention to sensations and thoughts. Those are the most noticeable distractions. You identify sensations and thoughts that distract you from your center. As you do this, your speed of awareness increases, and you are able to notice more subtle sensations and thoughts. This can often yield surprises, especially in the thoughts that you notice. Many of these thoughts are not ones you will be proud of. You will ask yourself, "Did I really think that?" It is important simply to accept distressing thoughts and disengage from them, without blaming yourself or feeling guilty.

One of the other things you will notice is that thoughts, sensations, and emotions have a life of their own. They will arise and disappear spontaneously, and one will lead into another without any input from you. This will teach you that much of what you consider to be your "self" is really just a number of programmed reactions. As you become aware of these, you gain the ability to change them. You can respond instead of react.

Attending differs from centering because you identify distractions precisely when you are attending, instead of ignoring them. When you are attending, your goal is to identify other phenomena, not just to stay aware of your center. Attending trains your mind to go out, touch something, and then come back; this builds pliancy. Many times you must identify thoughts or feelings that you would rather ignore—this builds warmth.

Basic attending skills can be developed in a few weeks. However, because attending gives you enormous amounts of information about yourself, it is something that you can continue to benefit from for years.

BRIAN'S FIRST EXPERIENCE WITH ATTENDING

Brian sits down for his morning meditation session. Today he is starting a new practice, attending. He was doing well at centering, and his teacher told him, *Once you can center for about thirty seconds without getting distracted, then you are ready to move on to the next practice, attending*. Brian focuses his intention by remembering his goals for meditation, and he recalls the immediate goal for this session: to center on sensations in his nose while identifying and disengaging from distractions.

Brian notices the sensations of air moving in and out of his nose. He feels the sense of coolness as he breathes in, and the sense of warmth as he breathes out. These sensations are rather faint, and he finds them a little difficult to keep track of. He suddenly gets distracted by an itch on his leg. He identifies the sensation as an itch and disengages from it by moving his attention back to the sensations of air moving in and out of his nose.

Almost immediately he feels the itch again. He identifies the sensation and brings his awareness back to the air moving in and out of his nose. Again the itch distracts him. Brian feels frustrated by this. He identifies his experience as frustration, and goes back to the sensations of his breath. The itch returns and Brian identifies it and goes back to his breath. He wonders if he is getting anywhere. He identifies this as a thought and goes back to the sensations of his breath moving in and out of his nose. The itch returns. Brian remembers, *It is OK to move or shift position to relieve discomfort, especially when you are beginning. Just make sure, before you shift or scratch or whatever, that you have identified what is causing you to want to move. As your skill improves, you will get better at disengaging from distractions, and that will keep you from getting frustrated.* Brian identifies the itch and moves his hand and scratches it. He feels a sense of relief and then goes back to focusing on the sensations of air moving in and out of his nose.

Brian figures that he has been sitting for less than two minutes and already he feels exhausted. He remembers the sense of peace he felt from centering and wonders if attending is going to be of any use to him. *Attending can take more effort than centering. Therefore it can feel more tiring, especially at first. It is a critically important practice because it develops mental pliancy, the ability to identify and disengage, and the ability to contain emotions. If you only practice centering, you may feel relaxed, but you will not make much progress.*

Brian identifies these thoughts and moves his awareness back to his breath. He continues to be distracted every couple of seconds and can't believe how noisy his mind is. He remembers a comment from his teacher, *Most of our mental noise goes unnoticed. When you first start to practice attending, you are often surprised by how noisy your mind really is.*

After a couple more minutes, Brian is feeling a sense of mental fatigue. He is wondering if he should stop meditating. *When you are feeling fatigued with a more advanced practice, then you should exert effort, but do not strain yourself. If you are feeling strain, then move to an easier practice. If you are feeling tired from attending, go back to centering for the remainder of the session. That is better than stopping the session early.*

Brian identifies these thoughts, and decides that he has expended enough effort for the day. He shifts his attention from the sensations of air moving in and out of his nose to the sensations in his lower abdomen. After a couple of breaths, he feels the usual sense of calm return and the distractions subside.

Soon his alarm beeps and he reflects on his experience. He notes how attending takes more effort than centering. His mind has to work differently when attending in order to identify and disengage from distractions. He is also surprised at how much noise his mind makes. He has a sense that he will be learning a lot from this practice. Brian brings his awareness to his whole body, he remembers the time and place, and then stretches his arms and legs as he opens his eyes.

MARIA'S FIRST EXPERIENCE WITH ATTENDING

Maria has practiced centering for two weeks. It has remained somewhat difficult for her after her initial success. However, she has reached the point where she can maintain continued awareness of the sensations in her lower abdomen for about thirty seconds before getting distracted. She wondered if she had made any real progress, but her teacher said, *You are doing fine. Once you can maintain continuous awareness of your center for twenty to thirty seconds without getting distracted, you are ready to move on to attending.*

Maria arrives home, changes out of her work clothes, goes into the garage, and sits in her car as she has done before. She adjusts her blanket over herself, closes her eyes, and focuses her intention for the session. She remembers her goals for meditation and then thinks about the immediate goal for this session: identifying distractions and disengaging from them while she centers on the sensations of air moving in and out of her nose.

The first thing Maria notices is that her nose is a bit stuffy and it feels hard to breathe through. The distraction is obvious, she can't get enough air. It is also very difficult to disengage her awareness from the sensation that she is suffocating. *If you nose is stuffed, or if it feels congested, then breathe through your mouth. Center on the sensations of air moving across your lips instead of the sensations of air moving in and out of your nose.*

Maria opens her mouth slightly and breathes more easily. She notices the coolness of the air as it flows in and the warmth as it flows out. After a couple of breaths, Maria realizes that she is thinking about work. She identifies those thoughts and disengages from them by deliberately bringing her awareness back to the sensations of air moving across her lips. She then feels a tingling in her left foot. She identifies it as a tingling and disengages her awareness from it, moving her awareness back to her lips. The tingling fades. Maria then senses how the coolness she feels at her lips as she inhales seems to flow inward through her mouth and down into her lungs. She begins to have a sense of the air flowing into her whole body. A comment from her teacher comes to mind, *When you start to practice attending, you want to center on something specific. Restrict your center to the sensations in your nose or lips. Do NOT focus on the sensations of the air moving through your body. That is a different exercise, and if you do it, you will not get the benefits from practicing attending.*

Maria brings her awareness back to the sensations of air moving across her lips. She again gets distracted by thoughts about work. She identifies these as "thoughts about work," and moves her awareness back to her lips. Then she remembers that one of her children had asked her to buy something, and she had forgotten about it. She recognizes this as a thought, and again centers her awareness on the sensations of air moving across her lips. The thought comes back immediately, and she identifies this as a "thought about forgetting" and places her awareness on the sensations at her lips. She begins to feel upset and identifies this as "feeling upset," and goes back to her breath. Then she feels her shoulders tighten. She notices this sensation, and goes back to centering on the sensations of air moving in and out of her mouth. Then the thoughts return about forgetting the purchase and how her child will react.

Maria feels like she is getting beaten up by the thoughts about having forgotten to buy the item for her child. She remembers a suggestion from her teacher, *If you are getting bombarded by repeated distractions related to the same topic, then one way of disengaging is to say "later" in your mind after you have identified the distractions. This tells your mind that you will deal with the issue, but that you have more important things to do now.*

Maria finds herself thinking about her child's reaction. She identifies those thoughts and thinks, "later." She goes back to the sensations at her lips. This seems to quiet her mind a bit. She is able to stay centered on her breath for a little bit, and then the thoughts about forgetting the item for her child return. She recognizes these and again thinks, "later." The thoughts go away, and Maria is able to return her awareness to the sensations of air moving across her lips.

Maria feels a little tired from the experience, but she also feels a sense of relief from having quieted the thoughts about her child.

A feeling of calm and peace comes over her, and she is able to keep her awareness on the sensations in her mouth as she breathes. She continues to identify distractions as they arise and to return her awareness to her breath in a calm manner, until she hears her watch alarm beep.

As Maria reflects on her experience, she first notices that it seemed easier to identify the distractions in this attending practice than to ignore them the way she did in her centering practice. She was also pleased at how thinking "later" seemed to quiet her mind. Finally, she realizes that she feels much calmer about having forgotten the item for her child, and will be able to handle her child's disappointment more peacefully. Instead of getting upset and berating herself for being so forgetful and uncaring, she feels that she can simply accept the situation and apologize calmly. Maria then brings her awareness to her whole body, she reorients to time and place, and then wiggles her fingers and toes a bit as she opens her eyes.

THE BASICS OF ATTENDING

Attending teaches you to identify and disengage from mental phenomena. The basic attending technique builds on centering, but differs from it. During centering practice, you ignore distractions: if you lose the awareness of your center, then you simply move your awareness back to it. During attending practice, you identify distractions clearly, and then disengage from them and go back to being aware of your center.

In order to identify a distraction, you accept the fact that your awareness is not on your center. You do not try to hold on to your center. You accept the distraction into your awareness and simply classify it as a thought, a sensation, or an emotion.

By accepting the distraction without fighting it, you develop the mental quality of warmth. Your mind becomes more accepting of phenomena.

You want to identify the distractions simply. You do not want to analyze them. At first, you only need to distinguish between thoughts, sensations, and emotions. Many people find that they can identify the distractions more precisely than that, and as long as you are not analyzing the distractions, you may do so. Brian labeled a sensation as an itch, and Maria was able to notice a thought about her child. However, both Brian and Maria made those identifications immediately. They did not have to think about them.

After identifying a distraction, you must disengage from it and move your awareness back to your center. This deliberate movement of your awareness develops mental pliancy. Your mind becomes more flexible.

In order to disengage from a distraction, you often must exert some effort. It is more active than simply "letting go." Often, the distractions grab your attention like a thornbush grabs clothing. Letting go does not remove the thorns from your clothes, nor does it remove the distractions from your experience. To remove the thorns, you must notice each one and work it loose from your clothing. To disengage from distractions, you must deliberately identify each and work your awareness away from it. This can take practice.

One way to disengage from distractions is simply to exert the mental effort required to move your awareness back to your center. If the distractions keep returning, then saying "later" in your mind can help. This works well for thoughts about a problem, because you let your mind know that you will not neglect the issue, but will get to it in time.

If the distraction is an uncomfortable sensation, then it is all right to disengage from the distraction by moving or shifting to relieve the discomfort. Just make sure that you have identified the sensations and that you move deliberately, with awareness, instead of reacting automatically.

One of the most helpful techniques for disengaging easily is to catch distractions earlier and identify them more quickly. The distractions can be thought of as a net with a lot of fishhooks attached. If you do not see the net coming, then by the time you notice it, it may be wrapped around you, and you will have several hooks embedded in you. If you notice the net coming quickly, you can deflect it before any of the hooks have sunk into you. Then you do not get caught by it. The following story, told by Joe, illustrates this.

I was starting a meditation session at about 11:00 p.m. I had planned to do a rather complex practice, and I had waited until the house was quiet so that I wouldn't be disturbed by noise. As soon as I started, a neighbor's dog began to bark. The sound was very distracting and I quickly became quite irritated, first at the dog, and then at the neighbor who was not doing anything to stop the noise. I identified the emotions as irritation and frustration, and moved my awareness back to what I wanted to practice. Then the dog barked again, distracting me. I recognized the distraction as a dog barking, but then I experienced angry thoughts and irritation. I kept trying to disengage from them, but the irritation and angry thoughts returned with a vengeance.

Since I was having difficulty disengaging from those emotions, I sped up my mental awareness to identify the distractions more precisely. The most obvious distraction was the barking dog; I realized, however, that it was not a sensation, but a perceptual conclusion. I really had no proof that there was any dog barking. It could have been a tape recorder playing the sound of a dog barking. So I worked on being more precise. As I did so, I became aware that the distraction was some sensation in my ears that came and went and rose and fell. There was no bark, and no dog. That sensation was quite easy to disengage from, and I was able to continue the practice I had intended at the start of the session.

By learning to identify and disengage from distractions, you develop mental pliancy and warmth. In this basic attending technique, you train yourself to identify and disengage from distractions while centering on the sensations of air moving in and out of your nose. When you center on the sensations in your nose, you are not stimulating your mind to produce any particular distractions. If you center on other things, the distractions will often be different. In part II, where we describe applications of meditation, you will see how attending while centering on other things generates more specific distractions that lead to insight into your life.

INSTRUCTIONS FOR EXTENDED ATTENDING PRACTICE

1. Sit in a comfortable place where you are not likely to be disturbed. It is all right if there are some distractions, as distractions are useful during attending.
2. Focus your intention by thinking about your long-range goals for meditation, and your immediate goal for the session. Your immediate goal for this exercise is to center on the sensations of air moving in and out of your nose while you identify and disengage from distractions.

3. Notice the sensations of air moving in and out of your nose. Keep your awareness on the sensations in your nose, and do not follow the sensations of air moving inward. The most obvious sensations are a sense of coolness as you inhale and warmth as you exhale.
4. Breathe comfortably; there is no need to change your breathing pattern. Note that your breathing pattern may vary during the exercise.
5. If you get distracted from the sensations in your nose, identify what distracted you. To identify the distraction, notice the distraction enough so that you can recognize it. There is no need to use mental descriptions of the distraction or to talk to yourself about what it was. You have identified the distraction if you could describe it if you were shaken by the shoulder and asked what distracted you. The distraction typically will be either a sensation or a thought (sometimes an emotion is the distraction, but that seems to be less common).
6. After identifying the distraction, disengage your awareness from it by moving your attention back to your center—the sensations of air moving in and out of your nose. Disengaging from the distraction may take some effort. One way of disengaging is simply to refocus your awareness on the sensations in your nose after identifying the distraction. This will work for most distractions.
7. If the same distraction keeps returning, telling it "later" after identifying it can help you disengage from it. Identifying the distraction as quickly as possible will also help you disengage from it.
8. Another way of disengaging is to identify the activity of your mind, instead of the content. For example, if you

are having difficulty disengaging from a thought, you can recognize that activity as "thinking," instead of identifying the content of the thought. Recognizing the activity separates you from the content of the thoughts, making it easier to disengage from them. In the same way, if you are being distracted by sensations, you can identify the activity as "sensing," and if emotions are causing the difficulty, you can recognize that activity as "feeling."

9. Continue to identify any distractions and to return your awareness to your center for the rest of the exercise.

When you practice this technique, you may find yourself distracted every couple of seconds. This is normal; simply continue to identify and disengage from the distractions. If you begin to feel too tired, stop attending and simply center on the sensations in your lower abdomen—that will be more peaceful. Remember, your endurance will increase with practice.

Before you end the session, reflect on your experience. After the session, you may want to make notes about any distractions that seemed important. Do not try to make notes during the session.

When you can identify distractions and disengage from them without straining for two to three minutes out of the fifteen minute session, then you will be ready to add the next practice—concentrating.

BRIEF ATTENDING PRACTICE

The extended attending technique described above should be practiced for at least fifteen minutes at a time. There is a brief technique to increase attending skills that must be practiced as well. This brief technique is incredibly useful, and will increase your understanding of how your mind works. The technique takes less than thirty seconds and can be done anytime and anywhere, except while operating machinery.

To do the brief technique, you ask yourself, "What's going on, and how did I get here?" You then pay attention to what is on your mind, and what has been going through it for the previous couple of minutes. After reviewing the thoughts, sensations, and emotions that you have experienced over the last couple of minutes, you stop the technique and go on with your activity.

You should do this technique several times per day. You may be surprised at some of the patterns that run through your mind on a regular basis, even when you are not feeling particularly emotional. The technique is quite useful if you are feeling upset, anxious, fearful, or sad. Then you can often get some ideas about how to handle your negative emotion in a constructive manner.

Remember, this is a brief technique. It should take you only a few seconds to review the last couple of minutes of your experience. If you are spending more than that, then you are getting too analytical, or reviewing too far back in time. Keep it short.

Brian's Experience with Brief Attending Practice

Brian is sitting at his desk at work. He suddenly realizes that his neck is feeling stiff. He remembers, *The brief attending technique is to be practiced frequently throughout the day. It is especially good to practice if you notice yourself feeling tense or upset*. Brian decides that this is a good time to practice, as he is definitely tense for some reason. Brian's intention is to be aware of his experience and where it comes from. He asks himself the question, "What is going on?" He tunes in to his current experience and notices the tension in his neck and shoulders. As he does so, he thinks about what has happened over the last couple of minutes. He remembers that he had just seen a memo from his supervisor in his morning mail. He remembers that he then thought about a project he was a little behind on. His mind had jumped to the conclusion that the memo was going to be asking him for an immediate report on the project. He then remembers that his shoulders and neck tensed as he thought about how he would have to explain why he was behind on the project. Brian reflects on how his tension is related to a conclusion that he made without any actual data. The whole technique has taken about ten seconds. Brian decides to look at the memo right away, so that he can deal with it instead of worrying about it. As he reads it, he sees that it is just a reminder of a meeting he is to attend later that day. Brian laughs to himself, and feels his neck and shoulders relax a bit. He decides that it would be a good idea to take a minute and relax. He closes his eyes and does the brief centering practice he enjoys, thinking "calm" as he breathes in and "relaxed" as he breathes out. After a minute, he reflects on how comfortable he feels and how much more energy he seems to have. He returns to his work with a sense of satisfaction.

Several hours later, Brian is walking down the hall toward the copy machine. He feels curious about what is on his mind and decides to do the brief attending practice. He sets his intention to pay attention to what is going on in his mind. As he checks in with himself, he realizes that he is thinking about an upcoming basketball game. Observing his thoughts over the last minute, he realizes that he started thinking about a game he had watched on television the previous week, and then began thinking about the upcoming game, wondering who would win, given what he had seen last week. There doesn't seem to be any particular reason for his thinking about the games, his mind was just doing it spontaneously. He reflects on the experiences and decides, correctly, that this was just some random noise going through his mind, which has no particular meaning. The brief session takes about fifteen seconds, and he finishes it as he gets to the copy machine.

Several days later, Brian is at home. He returned from work a short while ago, and is having to deal with some squabbling between his children. He suddenly realizes that he feels very irritable. He focuses his intention to be aware of his experience and asks himself, "What's going on?" He notices a series of angry thoughts about his family not appreciating him. As he becomes aware of his sensations, he realizes that his physical energy is low and he feels a little lightheaded. He suddenly remembers that he skipped lunch to get more work done. He reflects on the fact that this may have something to do with his being irritable. Brian tells his children that he will be right back. He goes to the bathroom and washes his face, and then goes to the refrigerator and gets a glass of juice. His head feels much clearer and he has more energy now. He returns to the living room and deals with the conflict between his kids without getting angry.

Maria's Experience with Brief Attending Practice

Maria is driving to work, when she suddenly notices that she is anxious. While at a stop light, she decides to do her brief attending practice. She sets her intention to be aware of what is going on in her mind. She asks herself the question, "What's happening?" She notices her anxiety, and then realizes that she is thinking about getting a ticket. She suddenly remembers that she just saw a police car pull out from a side street. Maria is surprised that simply seeing a police car made her so nervous. She starts to think about that, but remembers, *When you do the brief practice, you will be amazed at some of the things your mind comes up with. Don't try to analyze them. Just notice them and keep the practice short.* Maria reflects that she has been driving well and so is in no danger of getting a ticket. She also decides to pay some extra attention to her driving as she completes her trip to work. A few seconds later, the light turns green and she moves on.

Later, Maria is walking out of the office building on her way to lunch. She decides to do the brief attending technique and asks herself, "What am I thinking?" She realizes that she is thinking about gardening. She then remembers her experience over the last couple of minutes. When she left her work, she had noted that it was a nice spring day. Then she had seen buds on a tree, and heard a bird chirping. That made her think about winter being over and spring being a time for planting, which led to her thoughts about gardening. As she reflects on this, she notes that this thought sequence was just a natural response to her environment. As the thoughts are pleasant, she continues to think about the garden that she wants to plant while she walks the rest of the way to lunch.

A couple of days afterward, Maria has the sense that a headache is coming on. She decides to check in with herself, and asks, "What's my experience?" She notices the sensations in her head, and then notices some thoughts concerning a disagreement with a friend at work. Maria recalls that thoughts about the disagreement came up during several brief attending sessions over the last couple of days. She reflects on how she needs to work on reaching an understanding of her friend's position. She decides to call her friend that afternoon to schedule some time to talk. As

Maria finishes the brief practice, she notices that her body feels different. Her head feels a little more comfortable. Since she does feel some discomfort, she decides to take a mild pain reliever to prevent any more severe symptoms from developing.

Brief Practice—"What's Going On?"

The brief attending practice is incredibly useful and develops the mind rapidly. It takes only a few seconds, and should be limited to that amount of time. Its purpose is to make you aware of your current experience, and prompt you to remember what has gone through your mind for the previous couple of minutes. You are not to analyze your experience, but simply observe it.

INSTRUCTIONS FOR BRIEF ATTENDING PRACTICE

1. Focus your intention to be aware of your immediate experience.
2. Ask yourself the question, "What's going on?"
3. Attend to your immediate experience.
4. Notice what other sensations, thoughts, or emotions come to mind.
5. Trace these experiences back over the previous couple of minutes. Remember what you saw, felt, thought, or did during that time, and note how one thing led to another.
6. Simply note the flow of your experiences; do NOT analyze where the experiences came from. This is especially important for people who have had experience with psychology. You should NOT be psychoanalyzing

yourself. All you should be doing is observing the flow of your experience over the previous couple of minutes.
7. After a few seconds, stop and reflect on what you have observed. Note any associations that seem important.

This exercise should be done several times per day. It is especially important to do this if you feel a sudden change in mood or body sensation.

After doing the brief attending exercise, you may decide to take some action. Brian did a brief centering exercise to reduce the stress from the memo he saw. He washed his face and got a glass of juice when he realized he was hungry. Maria decided to call her friend rather than ignore their disagreement any longer.

BRIAN AND MARIA'S PROGRESS AFTER ONE MONTH OF PRACTICING ATTENDING

Brian is sitting down for a meditation session to practice attending. He has been practicing attending while centering on the sensations of air moving in and out of his nose for about four weeks. It was difficult for him at first, but he is more comfortable with it now. Brian focuses his intention by remembering his goals for meditation, and centers on the sensations of air moving in and out of his nose. He notes some tension in his shoulder, and disengages from it, moving his awareness back to the sensations in his nose. He then identifies the thought, "You're tense today," and disengages from it. The thought returns, and he disengages from it again, going back to feeling the air moving in and out of his nose. The thought returns, and Brian identifies his mind's activity as "thinking." This makes the thought "You're tense" seem more distant. He is able to disengage from it and go back to being aware of his center. Then his mind settles down for a few breaths. Brian notes that the distractions are much easier to disengage from. He identifies this as a thought, and goes back to being aware of his breath.

Brian continues to identify and disengage from distractions smoothly for the next few minutes. He finds that this takes effort, but it is not straining him. Suddenly, he remembers that he has a dentist appointment that afternoon. He identifies this thought, but when he tries to move his awareness back to the sensations in his nose, he can't quite feel them. He is having numerous thoughts about his dental appointment. They seem to have grabbed his attention and won't let go. He tries to identify the thoughts, but there are too many and they are coming too fast. Brian realizes that he needs to do something else to disengage from these thoughts. He asks himself what his mind is doing, and labels the activity as "thinking." After telling himself that he is thinking a couple of times, he feels the intensity of the thoughts decrease. It feels like he has some distance from them. He is then able to disengage from them by moving his awareness back to his breath. He then identifies and disengages from several distractions in rapid succession: a feeling of anxiety, some tension in his neck, a thought about his neck being tense, some tension in his left shoulder, the feeling of anxiety again. After another minute, he is back to simply being calmly aware of the sensations of air flowing in and out of his nose.

Brian remembers some of the thoughts he was having about the dentist. He is tempted to analyze them to figure out why they might have been so intense. However, he remembers a warning from his teacher, *As you practice attending, you can get fascinated by how thoughts, sensations, and emotions all flow from one into the other. Avoid analyzing them. Just continue to observe the flow during the practice. Any analysis should be done during the reflection stage of the session, or later in the day. The purpose of attending is to train your ability to be aware and accepting of what your mind produces*. Brian identifies this thought, and goes back to being calmly aware of the sensations in his nose.

A few minutes later Brian's watch beeps at him, signaling the end of the session. As Brian reflects on his experience, he remembers the intense thoughts about the dentist, and notices that they were mostly about being in the dentist's chair. He realizes that his discomfort comes from the experience of not being able to talk, not being able to say "stop" if his dentist is causing him pain. He decides that he will set up a hand signal with his dentist that will mean "That hurts. Stop, I want to say something to you." He then feels a lot more comfortable about his upcoming appointment.

Brian also reflects on how attending is quite different from centering. It is a lot more work for him, but it also yields a lot more information. The attending practice seems to sharpen his mind. His mind moves more fluidly and more quickly as he identifies fleeting thoughts and sensations, and then disengages and goes back to centering on the sensations in his nose. He is also becoming aware of how sensations, thoughts, and emotions influence each other. Brian feels that he is ready for the next practice, and decides that he will talk to his teacher about it.

Maria is sitting for her afternoon meditation session, after about four weeks of attending practice. She enjoys attending very much, and has continued to practice it even though she felt that she could have gone on to the next practice a week ago. She focuses her intention, and centers on the sensations of air moving in and out of her nose. Her mind is much calmer than it used to be, and there is much less mental noise. As thoughts come up and distract her, Maria identifies them quickly and goes back to her breath. She has the feeling that her mind is moving lightly from her breath to the distraction, and then back to her breath. This sense of lightness in her mind is enjoyable; it keeps her from feeling caught by distressing thoughts. Along with this lightness comes a feeling of greater control over her mind. As Maria continues to sit, she is distracted by a distressing thought about a difficult situation at work. She identifies the thought, but it returns. Maria continues to center on her breath, and deliberately pays more attention to the sensations of air moving in and out of her nose. As she does this, she is again distracted by the thought about work. She identifies this activity as "thinking." She notes how the activity of thinking feels different from the activity of being aware of the sensations in her nose. Noticing this difference helps her to disengage from the thoughts about work. She is able to move her awareness back to the sensations of air moving in and out of her nose.

When her alarm chimes at the end of the session, Maria reflects on how she enjoys attending practice. It is much easier to identify distractions and disengage from them than it was to ignore them, as she tried to do during centering practice. She had asked her teacher why she couldn't have just started with attending, and he had responded, *You must know how to center before you begin attending, because you need to have a center to go back to. Otherwise, you will not experience the back and forth movement of the mind. Your mind will just jump around from one thing to another, and that will not be as helpful.*

Maria considers how this practice has reduced her feeling of being scattered. Instead of experiencing her mind jumping around like a Ping-Pong ball, she feels it moves more fluidly. It is like a flexible tree that can move freely, but always comes back to its original position. Her mind is receptive, but less reactive.

Maria has also learned that as she simply identifies thoughts and sensations and emotions over time, they change and may even go away. As Maria identifies the distractions, she can easily separate individual sensations and thoughts. She has a sense of how an emotion will sometimes distract her, and how that emotion is related to the thoughts going through her mind. Maria would like to continue to practice attending, but she remembers, *You will find that certain practices are more enjoyable than others. That is because your mind's natural abilities fit with certain practices. Your natural pliancy and warmth make attending enjoyable. However, if you just practice what is easy for you, you will not develop the mental qualities you are lacking. You need to move on to the next practice. You will continue to practice attending, but not in every session.*

Maria has been using the brief attending practice several times per day. She finds herself asking "What's going on?" fairly spontaneously. She has gotten used to being surprised by the thoughts and images that arise when she does this practice. Many of them are bizarre, and they tend to be fearful and anxious. While they are somewhat based on reality, they present scenarios that are very unlikely ever to come about. She has learned to just accept these, and to avoid getting upset over them. She even has a sense of humor about this, a "there I go again" attitude. This keeps her on a more even keel throughout the day.

About three weeks after she began to practice attending, Maria discovered a way to use attending practice to relax, and to help her fall asleep. One night, Maria was lying in bed, unable to sleep because of incessant thinking. She decided to just start paying attention to how her body was feeling. She lay still and centered on her breath, while identifying and disengaging from distracting thoughts. After a couple of minutes, the thoughts began to slow down and become less bothersome. Maria then moved her awareness to her left foot. She centered on the sensations in her toes and foot while disengaging from distracting thoughts. After a bit, she moved her awareness up to her ankle. She felt how the toes, foot, and ankle were all connected, and how the sensations differed in each. If other thoughts entered her mind, she simply identified them and went back to focusing on the sensations. Maria continued to move her center of awareness upward until she was aware of her whole left leg. As she did this, her thoughts became fewer and quieter. She then repeated the process with her right leg. Once she had finished both her legs, she moved her awareness into her hips, pelvis, and then up into her abdomen. She hadn't quite finished becoming aware of her abdomen when she fell asleep.

When Maria asked her teacher about this, he was pleased. *Good for you. You are playing with the techniques, and figuring out how to apply them. You centered on different areas of the body in turn while attending to sensations and thoughts. This can be very relaxing and, if done at bedtime, can often help you get to sleep. You can also use this as a relaxation exercise at other times.*

Brian and Maria are both ready to move on to the next practice. Maria is more comfortable than Brian with the attending practice, because it uses her naturally strong mental qualities of pliancy and warmth. Both of them are experiencing benefits of increased insight and awareness. They are also more aware of constructive ideas and thoughts throughout the day. Their moods are generally more positive, and they are more able to change their mental state when they are upset. They are more accepting of themselves, and this helps them to be more accepting of others.

CONCLUSION

Attending consists of identifying and disengaging from mental contents as they arise. The mental contents can be thoughts, sensations, emotions, or combinations of these. Each item is identified and then disengaged from. In the beginning stages, attending is combined with centering; the center acts as an anchor to keep the mind from drifting off. The basic attending technique is to center on the sensations of air moving in and out of the nose and to attend to distractions. Anything that distracts you from being aware of your center is identified and then disengaged from, as you bring your attention back to the sensations of air moving in and out of your nose.

The disengagement process can take more effort than simply "letting go." Often, the distractions will have grabbed your mind, and letting go of them will not make them let go of you. Four ways of disengaging from the distractions follow.

- Exert effort, and deliberately pay attention to what you were centering on.
- Identify the distractions quickly, before they have a chance to entangle you.
- Tell the distraction "Later!" after you have identified it.
- Identify the mental activity that is associated with the distraction: sensing, thinking, or feeling.

You should practice the extended attending technique for periods of at least fifteen minutes, for a total of ninety minutes per week. A sign of success will be when you experience your mind easily going back and forth between your center and any distractions.

The brief attending technique—called "What's going on?"—consists of paying attention to what is going through your mind, several times per day. Each time, you should just observe the thoughts, sensations, and emotions that are on your mind, without analyzing them. The period of observation should last up to thirty seconds, and no more. This will help you be more aware of the background activity your mind is putting out during the course of the day.

Attending is like sitting on the bank of a river, watching what goes by. You want to identify what flows past as precisely as possible, without getting caught and pulled into the river. Sometimes objects on the river get caught in an eddy and take a while to move downstream. But eventually everything moves along.

You are ready to move on to the next practice when you can identify and disengage from distractions easily, without getting caught by them, for about two minutes at a time.

TIPS

Remember to focus your intention at the start of each extended session, by reviewing your intended results for meditation and the immediate purpose of the session. The immediate purpose of the extended attending technique is to identify and disengage from distractions, while centering on the sensations of air moving in and out of your nose. Setting your intention takes only a couple of seconds, but increases the effectiveness of your practice. Before executing the brief practice, set your intention simply to be aware of what is on your mind.

Alertness is very important in attending practice. Make sure that you stay awake during the sessions. Washing your face in cold water or sitting in a more upright position can help.

If you feel physical discomfort during a session and cannot seem to disengage from it, then it is all right to move to relieve the discomfort, as long as you first identify it precisely.

If you feel mental strain during a session, especially when you first start to practice attending, then stop doing the attending practice and just center on the sensations in your lower abdomen. This will keep you from straining your mind.

You can also use attending to relax. Center on different body areas in turn as you identify and disengage from other sensations, thoughts, or emotions. It is fine to do this at bedtime to help yourself fall asleep.

four

concentrating: sharpening the mind like a razor

•

Seek concentration, since insight with
concentration will destroy your delusions.

Shantideva

•

Concentrating is the third meditative practice you will learn. While you are learning it, you should intersperse your extended concentrating sessions with extended attending sessions. We recommend that you practice the extended attending technique for one out of three of your extended sessions. You will practice the extended concentrating technique during the other sessions. Practice only one technique per session; do not try to mix techniques during a single extended session.

When you practice concentrating, you will be focusing intently on a mental object. Concentrating uses the mental steadiness that you built up by your centering practice. Though it will further increase that steadiness, its main purpose is to develop your mental clarity. The mental clarity that you develop by practicing concentrating will complement the mental warmth that you developed by practicing attending.

As your mental clarity increases, you mind will become better at remembering and analyzing. You will find that you are able to remember precise details more easily. When you are faced with a complex problem, you will find that you are better able to perceive and analyze the different elements of the problem. You will think more clearly about complex issues.

In addition to improving your abstract reasoning skills, concentrating also improves your memory of recent events. One useful consequence of this is that you will always be able to remember where you have left your car keys.

Concentrating requires that you focus your awareness intensely on a mental object. The requirement to focus on a mental object is a critically important point. It is the process of stabilizing and perceiving the details of a mental object that develops your mental clarity. Focusing intensely on a physical object will not develop mental clarity. It will lead to some pleasant trance states and will develop mental steadiness, but it will not develop the clarity of mind that you will need to truly benefit from meditation.

The basic concentrating technique involves the following steps.

- Observing a simple physical object so that you will be able to remember it. (We recommend that you start by looking at a key.)
- Closing your eyes and allowing the memory of the object to appear in your mind. (Seeing the image of the key in your mind.)
- If something different appears in your mind, or if you lose track of the memory, refreshing your memory by observing the object again. (Looking at the key.)

- Repeating the last two steps for the rest of a session. It is unusual for anyone who is beginning concentrating practice to be able to focus clearly on the mental image of an object for more than a couple of seconds at a time.

Almost everyone has difficulty seeing the image of the key in their mind at first, but most people improve with practice. Some people, however, do not improve. The object remains just as difficult to visualize after one week as when they started. These people should work with the memory of a sound, by humming a note to themselves and then allowing the memory of the sound to appear in their mind. Some people will find it as difficult to make progress with the memory of a sound as with an image. They should work with the memory of a movement, by closing and opening their hand and then allowing the memory of the movement to appear in their mind.

The difficulty that some people have with visual and auditory memory seems to relate to preferred learning styles. It is commonly known that each person has a preferred learning style. For some people it is visual, others auditory, and still others kinesthetic. A visual learner would learn a set of instructions best by seeing them; an auditory learner would learn them best by listening to them; and a kinesthetic learner would learn them best by being taken through a physical activity that uses them.

There seems to be a loose relationship between a person's preferred learning style and the type of memorized image that they find easiest to concentrate on. Visual learners do best concentrating on visual images, auditory learners do better concentrating on memorized sounds, and kinesthetic learners do better concentrating on memorized movements. Since most people are visual learners, we ask people first to concentrate on a simple memorized image. If they have too much difficulty with that, then we have them work with a memorized sound, or a memorized movement.

The only way to succeed at concentrating is to be patient with yourself. (A sense of humor also helps.) Many times your mind does everything but concentrate on the image. Finally, you have a little success. The image appears. Then, just as you are feeling hopeful, the image changes or disappears. If you are patient and can laugh at the silly things that your mind does, you will be able to keep practicing. If you keep practicing, then you will improve, just as we ourselves did.

BRIAN BEGINS CONCENTRATING

Brian is beginning his morning meditation session. It is his first session practicing concentrating. He sits comfortably, focuses his intention, and looks at the key he has in his hand. It is a very old house key. Brian holds the key flat in his palm and examines it. He notes the bronze color of the key and its shape. He notes how the shape changes from one end of the key to the other. After examining the key for about a minute, he closes his eyes and waits for the image of the key to appear in his mind.

At first, nothing happens. All he is aware of is a sort of reddish color with dark splotches. He assumes that this is what his eyes see of the back of his eyelids. He continues to wait expectantly. Suddenly he sees the image of the key. But when he concentrates on the image, all but the tip of the key disappears. Brian squints his eyes trying to see where the other part of the key went. That causes the tip of the key to disappear too. Brian strains harder, trying to see the key. He then remembers, *Resist the temptation to use your eyes to look for the mental image of the key. Just let the image appear in your mind. Your eyes should feel totally relaxed. It is normal for the image to come and go, or to appear in bits and pieces. If you lose track of the image, just open your eyes and refresh your memory.*

Brian realizes that the image of the key is completely gone, so he opens his eyes and looks at the key again. After a few seconds, he closes his eyes and waits for the image to appear in his mind. This time it comes quickly, but it is pointing in a different position. Brian tries to rotate the image in his mind and feels like he is straining his neck. *Accept the image your mind produces, and concentrate on it. Do not try to manipulate it at this early stage. If the position changes, just observe the details clearly.*

Brian begins to realize that concentration is different from control. He opens his eyes again and looks at the key. Then he closes his eyes and waits for the image to appear in his mind. Again he gets bits and pieces of it. Suddenly he perceives the whole key as if he were looking at it. Then, just as he realizes that, the image fades. The exercise is frustrating him. *It can be very difficult to stabilize a mental image, even a simple one. In fact, if you can maintain the image of the key for more than a couple of seconds at a time, you are doing well. In order to succeed at concentrating, be patient with yourself and refresh your memory by frequently opening your eyes and looking at the key in your hand. It is OK to do that every minute if you need to.*

Brian allows himself a mental groan and opens his eyes again to look at the key. This time when he closes them, he finds a partial image of the key appears quickly. Instead of trying to make the rest of the key appear, he just concentrates on the part that has appeared. He notes with surprise that he is aware of a couple of details in the image that he was not aware of seeing on the key in his hand. He opens his eyes to check on this and sees that the image in his mind was correct. He is pleased, and closes his eyes again.

Images of bits and pieces of the key appear and disappear for the rest of Brian's meditation session. When his alarm goes off, he feels a sense of relief, and reflects on how difficult this simple exercise is. He also realizes that it will be a lot easier if he accepts the difficulty, and frequently opens his eyes to look at the key. He decides that he should take the advice of his teacher by accepting what happens and trusting that he will improve over time.

MARIA BEGINS CONCENTRATING

Maria is beginning her first session of concentrating. She focuses her intention, and then looks at her car key, which she is holding in front of her. She examines the flat side of the key, noting as many details as she can. As she notices more and more details, she wonders how she will ever remember them all and starts to feel overwhelmed. *You need not consciously memorize all the details of the object. Your mind is aware of them, and will recall them for you with practice.*

Maria then closes her eyes, and waits for the image of the key to appear in her mind. After a bit, her mind becomes noisy with random thoughts. Maria identifies these as thoughts and goes back to waiting for the image of the key to appear. She realizes that she has forgotten what it looked like. This is irritating, and she notes her mind scolding her. She remembers her teacher's words, *Be gentle with yourself. If you lose track of the mental image of the key, the solution is to open your eyes and refresh your memory. Getting upset or scolding yourself will just slow you down. So, when you have difficulty, simply open your eyes and refresh your memory.*

Maria opens her eyes, looks at the key again for a few seconds, and closes her eyes. After a bit, she suddenly realizes that the outline of the key has appeared. It seems to be somewhere above her head. She wonders if it should be in front of her, but it doesn't seem to want to move. *The image is to appear in your mind. Since you are not using your eyes, the image at first may seem to appear anywhere. Common places are in front of your eyes, inside your head, or above your head. Don't worry about where the image appears, just observe the details.*

Maria looks at the outline, but no other details appear. She opens her eyes again to refresh her memory. This time, after she closes her eyes, she perceives the image of the key in front of her—but it is rotating slowly in a counterclockwise direction. When she tries to stop this rotation, the image begins to rotate about its long axis, showing her first an edge and then a flat side in turn. *Just observe the details of the image that appears in your mind. Do not try to force the image in your mind to behave in any particular way.* Maria watches the key rotate and then fade away.

Maria refreshes her memory again, closes her eyes, and finds herself seeing the image of the family's pet cat. The image is quite clear, and it seems as if the cat is in front of her. She waits, but no image of the key appears. The cat suddenly changes into a lamp, which then fades. Maria wonders if there is something wrong with her. The images seem a little bizarre. *While you wait for the image of the key to appear in your mind, sometimes your mind will produce other images. Just observe them, and continue to wait for the image of the key to appear. If you identify the images and disengage from them, without getting emotionally caught up with them, then eventually they will disappear. If the image of the key does not appear, then open your eyes and refresh your memory of it.* Maria smiles to herself, opens her eyes, looks at the key for a few seconds, and then closes her eyes again.

Maria continues to perceive random images throughout the rest of the session. Occasionally, she gets glimpses of the image of the key, but these are somewhat rare. She is able to stay relaxed, and simply identify and disengage from the other images. When her alarm goes off, she reflects on how her mind did seem to generate complete images, but it had a great deal of difficulty keeping the images still or producing the image that she wanted to concentrate on. When she feels frustrated with this, she remembers, *You can be pleased that your mind is producing images, even if they are not the images that you want. The ability of your mind to produce images at all is useful. Remember, you will improve with practice.* Maria lets out a sigh, reminds herself that patience is a virtue, reorients to her body, time, and place, and then opens her eyes.

THE BASICS OF CONCENTRATING

Concentrating involves focusing on a mental image and perceiving it in complete detail. It is very important to work with a mental image because concentrating on a physical object does not develop the mind in the same way. As you improve, your awareness will become more focused on the mental image, so that awareness of other objects fades.

When starting concentrating practice, the mental object used is the memory of a simple physical object. The object should also be emotionally neutral, not something with strong feelings attached to it. Brian and Maria are both using the memory of the image of a key. A key is a small, familiar object with enough detail to be challenging, yet not so much detail as to be overwhelming.

Concentrating is usually the most difficult practice at first. There are numerous types of difficulties that arise. Brian experiences the difficulty of seeing only one piece of the image at a time. He is able to see a part clearly, but his mind does not see the whole image. Maria has the difficulty of seeing other images than the one she wants to concentrate on. Fortunately, these difficulties decrease with practice. Patience is essential. The best way to deal with difficulties is just to refresh your memory by looking at the key again. The mind has a great deal of difficulty stabilizing mental images, but it rapidly improves with practice.

INSTRUCTIONS FOR EXTENDED CONCENTRATING PRACTICE

1. Sit in a comfortable place where you are not likely to be disturbed. Quiet is important, so find a setting with as few distractions as possible.
2. Focus your intention by thinking about your long-range goals for meditation, and your immediate goal for the session. Your immediate goal for this exercise is to concentrate on the mental image of a key.
3. Hold the key in your hand so that one of the flat sides is facing you. Gaze at the key gently, and observe the details of its shape, color, and any distinctive markings. Spend only about a minute doing this.
4. Close your eyes and remember the key, allowing the image to appear in your mind. It is very important to have the sense of allowing the image to appear. There should be no sense of straining your eyes, or squinting to see something.
5. If other images appear or distracting thoughts arise, simply identify and disengage from them, and go back to waiting for the image of the key to appear.
6. If the image of the key does not appear after a minute or so, simply open your eyes, look at the key in your hand for a few seconds, and then close your eyes again.

7. When any part of the key appears, concentrate on the details of the image. When the image fades (or if the image remains incomplete), open your eyes again and refresh your memory. It is better to stay relaxed, and open your eyes frequently, then to strain or force the image to appear.
8. Repeat the process of looking at the key, and then closing your eyes and waiting for its image to appear in your mind.

Patience is very important in this practice. If the whole image appears in your mind and you can observe the details for even one or two seconds, you are doing well. You may be surprised at how difficult such a simple practice is. Most people have to look at the key about every minute, on the average, when they start practicing. That is all right—by accepting what you *can* do, you will progress faster than if you try to force your mind to do what it cannot. Just keep opening your eyes, refreshing your memory, and then closing them again.

BRIEF CONCENTRATING PRACTICE

The extended concentrating technique described above should be done in sessions of at least fifteen minutes. There is also a brief concentrating technique that you will practice. This brief practice will rapidly improve your ability to concentrate, and improve your memory as well.

For the brief practice, you spend one or two minutes remembering an emotionally neutral event from earlier in the day. You should remember as many details from the event as you can. The details may be from more than one sense; you can remember sights, sounds, smells, touches, and movements. In addition to augmenting your mental clarity, this brief practice will improve your memory.

Brian's Experience with Brief Concentrating Practice

Brian is sitting in his living room on a Saturday afternoon. He has nothing in particular to do, and is enjoying a bit of relaxation. He remembers that he needs to practice brief concentrating. He focuses his intention to concentrate on the details of an emotionally neutral event from earlier in the day. He closes his eyes and tries to remember breakfast that morning. At first, he is surprised to find that he doesn't recall having breakfast. He knows that he ate breakfast, but the memory is not coming to him. He remembers that he ate cereal, and with that thought he recalls sitting down at the table with a bowl of cereal. He observes the details of the memory, the look of the cereal in the bowl, the feel of the bowl and the spoon in his hand, the smell and taste of the cereal, and his body posture as he ate. He sees his son coming in and sitting down at the table, and hears himself greet his son. Some of the details are clearer than others, but Brian just observes what he can. After a couple of minutes concentrating on breakfast, Brian reflects on the experience. He notes that some of the details were clear, but others, especially things in his peripheral vision, were not. He also realizes that he must have sounded rather gruff when he greeted his son. He was not upset with his son, and decides that he should work on speaking in a more gentle tone of voice. Brian yawns, stretches, and opens his eyes. The whole brief technique has taken about two minutes.

Maria's Experience with Brief Concentrating Practice

Maria is sitting at her desk at work. She remembers that she is to practice brief concentrating. She doesn't particularly like the extended concentrating exercises, and wonders if the brief practice is all that necessary. *Concentrating can be one of the most frustrating exercises for some people. But is also vital for complete development. The brief exercises will help you immensely.* Maria focuses her intention to remember an event from earlier in the day. She closes her eyes and tries to remember breakfast. Nothing appears in her mind. She knows that she ate breakfast, but she simply cannot recall doing so. Suddenly, she has the clear image of brushing her teeth before leaving for work. She can see herself putting the toothpaste on the toothbrush, feel the movement of putting the brush in her mouth, taste and smell the toothpaste, and even see her reflection in the mirror. She is pleased by the clarity of the memory, but wonders if she has done the practice correctly, since this was not the memory she had planned on. *When doing the brief practice, it is the clarity of the details that is important. If you access a memory that is different than you planned, that is OK. You will gain more control over time.* Maria reflects on how her mind does have the ability to perceive details in mental images—it just seems to have its own ideas about what images to perceive. She reminds herself to have patience. She then stretches her arms, wiggles her toes, and opens her eyes.

One evening, Maria wants to go to the store to buy milk. She looks in her purse, but her car keys are not there. She can't recall where she put them, and she starts to feel frustrated; "I'm always losing my car keys!" she thinks to herself. Then she decides to try using the brief concentrating practice to find her keys. She focuses her intention to remember what she did with her keys. She then closes her eyes and thinks about the last time that she knew she had her keys: she knew that she had them when she drove home from work. She sees herself take them out of the ignition, and feels herself holding them in her hand as she walks into the house. She then sees her daughter run up and give her a hug. She drops her purse but keeps hold of her keys while she hugs her daughter. Then the phone rings, and she puts down her daughter and drops the keys on the counter while she answers the phone. The call is for her husband; she remembers writing a message for him on a sheet of paper and putting it on the counter. Then she watches herself pick up her purse and put it away, but she does not see herself pick up her keys after she put them on the counter. Maria opens her eyes and walks over to the counter. Her keys are not in view, but on an inspiration, she lifts up the sheet of paper on which she wrote the message to her husband. Under it she sees her car keys. Maria laughs, and is pleased with her success.

INSTRUCTIONS FOR BRIEF CONCENTRATING PRACTICE

The brief concentrating technique involves spending a couple of minutes remembering an emotionally neutral event from earlier in the day. It is important for the event to be emotionally neutral, because you want your mind to perceive details clearly without getting caught up in emotional turmoil.

The instructions are as follows.

1. Focus your intention to remember an event from earlier in the day.

2. Close your eyes and remember the event. Notice all the sensory details that you can. (These include sight, hearing, smell, taste, touch, and kinesthetic sensations.)
3. If nothing comes to mind, then "prime" your mind by thinking about the event. While you think about the event, be alert for any images that arise.
4. Allow these to appear in your mind, and observe the details.
5. If a different event comes to mind than the one you intended, accept that, and observe the details.
6. After one or two minutes, reflect on what you have experienced, and open your eyes. (As you get better at this technique, you can practice it with your eyes open.)

Brian's Results from Concentrating

Brian is beginning a meditation session, after six weeks of practicing concentrating. The technique has become easier for him, and he feels relaxed as he focuses his intention. He remembers his goals for meditation, and his goal of using this session to concentrate on the mental image of the key. Brian opens his eyes briefly to glance at the key and refresh his memory of its shape. He has become so familiar with it that this takes only a couple of seconds. As he closes his eyes, he experiences a brief darkness, and then sees the image of the key as if it were floating in front of his face. The image appears quite clear and steady. He is vaguely aware of some thoughts in the back of his mind, but they do not seem to be distracting him. The image of the key seems to be getting brighter, and the details are even sharper. Brian also begins to have the impression that he can perceive more than just visual details about the key. He can feel the smoothness of its surface, he even has a sense of its weight and hardness. His mind moves along the key from the tip to the back, noticing each bump and ridge. Even as his awareness zooms in on the tiny details, Brian keeps an awareness of the whole key. The experience is fascinating. Brian feels a sense of mental clarity, as if there is almost nothing separating him from the key.

Suddenly he realizes that he has lost track of his surroundings, and indeed has no idea if he is even breathing. This jolts him a bit, and he becomes aware of his body sitting comfortably and breathing easily. Brian has lost track of time, and he wonders if his alarm went off without him hearing it. He struggles with this thought, and then just opens his eyes and checks his watch. He is astonished to find that only three minutes have passed, when it felt like it could have been hours. *When your mind gets absorbed in concentrating, it does not keep track of time. The experience is timeless. After you come out of concentrating, your mind comes up with some estimate of the amount of time that has passed. This estimate can be wrong, but just observe it and let it go. You also need not worry about concentrating and missing your alarm. Because you have been using the alarm to alert you to the end of a session for a couple of months, your mind will recognize it and inform you, even if you do not notice it consciously.*

Brian is excited and pleased by the experience. He closes his eyes again, expecting to have the key appear in the same detail. This time, however, nothing happens. He wonders what is wrong, and feels the beginnings of frustration. As he observes what is going on, he realizes that his excitement had jarred his body a little, it is no longer as relaxed. *Concentrating is easier when the body is relaxed. If you are excited or agitated, just center on your abdomen or do some other relaxing meditation until you settle down. Then go back to concentrating.* Brian decides to use the brief centering practice, which he finds quite relaxing. He thinks "calm" as he breathes in and "relaxed" as he breathes out. After a couple of minutes, he feels himself settle and his muscles loosen. Brian then seeks to recall the image of the key from his memory, and within a short time it appears again. His experience is not as detailed or absorbing this time, but he is able to hold the image steady. After a few seconds, the image fades, but he is able to recall it without opening his eyes. *The experience of concentrating is variable, especially in the beginning. Sometimes your experience is intense and you are absorbed in it, and other times the mental images are more ephemeral. Just accept the variability, and enjoy the experience that you do have.* The key appears and reappears in Brian's mind for the rest of the session. As he reflects on his experience, he notices that his mind feels curiously rested and invigorated. This is a pleasant sensation, and he rises from his sitting posture with a bounce in his step and a smile on his face.

Over the preceding six weeks, Brian has noticed a number of benefits from concentrating. His thinking is clearer at work, and the brief practice has helped him remember details from meetings and take better notes, improving his efficiency and lowering his stress. Brian is finding that he can focus more intently during his golf game: he is much more aware of details in his swing, and he is finding things to correct that he was previously unaware of. The brief practice has made him aware of how gruff he sounds around the house, and he is changing that by consciously speaking in a softer, warmer voice. Brian has also noticed some of the negative nonverbal cues he gives when he is upset at work. One of these is clenching his fist when talking with a subordinate. He is working on keeping his hand open when he talks, and this is helping him to stay calmer.

Brian has used the concentrating practice to help himself relax before going to sleep. He discovered that he could imagine scenes from vacations he had taken that were especially enjoyable. He found that imagining these scenes was quite peaceful. One night, when he was restless and could not get to sleep, he began to imagine a scene from a camping trip. As he concentrated on the scene, he found himself settling down and getting lost in it. Soon, he felt like he was dreaming, and the next thing that he remembered was waking up in the morning. He asked his teacher about this. *Concentrating practice will improve your ability to visualize. You have discovered a way to use the skill of visualization to help you get to sleep. We will use your increased ability to visualize as we work more specifically on the applications for meditation.*

Maria's Results from Concentrating

Maria has been practicing concentrating for several weeks. It has been difficult, for she has continued to have trouble seeing the key in her mind. Bits and pieces of it would appear, and then they would rapidly fade; and she continued to experience many distracting images. After a couple of weeks without any progress, she felt like she was straining very hard and getting nowhere. Her concentrating sessions were becoming exhausting, and she couldn't seem to help but strain her eyes in order to try to see the key more clearly. Maria asked her teacher for advice. *Some people have a difficult time seeing things in their mind, because they are not visual. These people do better concentrating on the memory of a sound or of a movement. Practice concentrating on the memory of a sound. Hum a note, and let the memory of the sound appear in your mind. If the sound does not appear in your mind, refresh your memory by humming the note again.*

Maria tried this and found it somewhat easier. However, it was still quite exhausting. Her teacher next suggested that she work with a kinesthetic memory. *Sit comfortably, and then close and open your right hand. Do this several times, paying attention to the sensation of movement. Notice how the position of the fingers and even the rest of the hand changes as you close and open your hand. After doing this several times, keep your hand still, and allow the memory of the movement to appear in your mind.* Maria found this easier; her mind seemed to be able to perceive and remember the kinesthetic sensations more easily then the sound of the note or the sight of the key.

Maria is now sitting down for an extended session of concentrating. It has been about eight weeks since she started practicing concentrating, and about four weeks since she started using kinesthetic sensations. Maria focuses her intention for the session, and allows herself to breathe easily for a few minutes to settle down. Then she closes and opens her right hand very slowly several times. As she closes the hand, she notes the tactile sensations as her fingers flex. She notes the sensations inside her hand, focusing more on them than on external sensations. After doing this several times, she leaves her hand open, and then remembers what it felt like to close and open her hand. Her mind seems very peaceful today, and suddenly she has the sense that her hand is actually opening and closing. The feeling is somewhat odd because she can't quite seem to figure out where the feeling is located. She is aware of her physical hand lying open in her lap, but she can also feel the same hand opening and closing. Maria focuses more intently on the imagined sensations of movement in her hand; as she does so, the awareness of her physical hand disappears.

Maria begins to feel a sense of warmth in this imaginary hand and an experience of deep comfort. Time seems to slow down, as she observes the imagined kinesthetic sensations of movement in her hand. The hand seems to be opening and closing in incredibly slow motion. Maria's awareness is absorbed by the sensations of movement. She feels a very pleasurable connection with this imaginary hand. Suddenly, Maria realizes that she has gotten lost in the exercise and has completely lost track of the time, the rest of her body, and her surroundings. This realization startles her, and she goes through a brief period of disorientation as she connects to the rest of her body. For a few moments, she has the sensation again that she has two right hands—this time, the imaginary one feels stronger than the real one. As she pays attention to her body, the feeling of the imaginary hand fades by joining with the feeling of her actual right hand. As she opens and closes her actual right hand, Maria notices that she seems much more aware now of the kinesthetic perceptions that occur during those movements. She is aware of enjoying the movement more than she ever has before. As Maria is noticing this, she hears her watch alarm go off. She is amazed that more than twenty minutes have gone by while she was absorbed in concentrating on the memory of her hand moving.

Maria reflects on this experience. She notes how kinesthetic perceptions are much easier for her to concentrate on than auditory or visual images. She also notes how this deep concentrating is giving her a new appreciation for her body. She enjoys her body more, and feels more comfortable inside of it. Maria takes some time to bring her awareness to the rest of her body. She then reorients to time and place in a gradual manner, making sure that she remembers her surroundings before she wiggles her fingers and toes and opens her eyes. *After being absorbed in an experience of concentrating, it is important to return to the normal waking state in a gentle manner. Of course, if you had to respond to an emergency, you would be able to do so quickly. However, if you have the time, it is much more gentle to your system to change states gradually. So, take some time to bring your awareness to the rest of your body, remember the day and the time, remember the place and your surroundings, and then wiggle your fingers and toes and take some deep breaths before you open your eyes.*

In spite of the difficulty she has had with concentrating, Maria is experiencing a number of benefits from the practice. She is thinking more clearly, and this helps her work through the details of complex situations more easily. She also has an increased awareness of her body's sensations. Often, when under stress, she would move quickly and somewhat erratically. Now, she is able to move more slowly and more smoothly, and this seems to keep her mental state more calm. Maria's husband has commented that she gets less upset with the children. Her memory for small tasks that she needs to accomplish during the day has improved. She is also able to remember ideas for work that occur at random times. In the past, she would often forget such ideas before she had a chance to write them down; now she is able to remember them.

CONCLUSION

Concentrating consists of focusing attention on a mental object with such intensity that all the details of the object are clearly perceived. The intensity of the focus can be so great that you may lose track of the outside world (that is, everything except the object). The practice starts by using the memory of a familiar object as the object of concentrating. Brian and Maria both began by concentrating on the memorized image of a key. If a visual memory proves too difficult, you can use the memory of a simple sound, or a simple movement, just as Maria did.

You should practice concentrating in this way for at least fifteen minutes at a time, for a total of sixty minutes per week. Concurrently, you should spend at least thirty minutes per week practicing attending.

Avoid any sense of mental strain—just allow the memory to appear in your mind, and refresh your memory with the object if the memory fades.

You are ready to move on when you can hold the mental image in its entirety steady for about ten seconds.

The brief concentrating technique (called "What happened then?") consists of remembering the details of an event from earlier in the day. You should spend up to two minutes remembering. Unlike the extended practice, you should remember the event using all your sensory modalities: sight, touch, hearing, smell, taste, and kinesthetic sensations.

The combination of the brief and extended practices will improve your ability to concentrate. You will also find that your memory improves, and that your ability to think about abstract concepts increases.

TIPS

Focus your intention at the start of each session.

If, at the beginning, you are not able to recall the visual image, make sure that you are using a simple enough image. Remembering the image of a key seems to be good for most people. However, some people need to start with something simpler. The image of a number, a letter, or a simple symbol is an easier item to start with.

If you cannot remember visual images at all, then use the memory of a simple sound, or a simple hand movement.

Patience is the most important virtue when learning to concentrate. When you begin, remind yourself that it doesn't matter how often you have to refresh your memory.

It is very important to avoid any sense that you are straining your eyes to make the image appear in your mind. If you feel any strain in your eyes, open them and look at the object to refresh your memory.

As you finish each session, reflect on your experience, and then gradually reorient yourself to your surroundings.

five

opening: moving your mind beyond all limits

When meditating on visual images becomes difficult and depressing, then connect to the expansive spaciousness of the mind for relief.

The Essence of the Middle Way

Opening is the technique that develops spaciousness. Spaciousness is the mental quality that complements the other four: steadiness, pliancy, warmth, and clarity. Spaciousness is the key to creativity; it enables us to organize our perceptions, thoughts, and other mental contents into completely new patterns. Opening techniques help our minds experience spaciousness directly, so that we become familiar with it. As we open and experience spaciousness, our perceptions change and we can think in completely new ways.

Experiencing spaciousness is like being in a boat—and then suddenly becoming a fish swimming in the ocean, or becoming a bird and flying away. A sense of freedom and joy comes with it—no matter where your body might be, your mind can still soar.

As you cultivate spaciousness, you will

- have more creative ideas;
- become better at finding solutions when you are stuck;

- see multiple perspectives to a situation;
- find yourself laughing more; and
- realize how much of what you worry about doesn't really matter.

Spaciousness can lead to leaps of intuition that free the mind from traps caused by excessive thinking. An example of this is illustrated by the following story, told by Lobsang.

When I was training at the Buddhist School of Dialectics in Dharamsala, India, I studied Buddhist teachings from five o'clock in the morning until about half past eleven at night. I did this every day, and became so engrossed in the pursuit of philosophical knowledge that it was my only activity for months. Every moment of my time was spent in learning how to think, analyze, and debate, and in memorizing more philosophical ideas.

One day, I took the afternoon off and walked to the waterfalls that cascaded down the mountains about a mile from the monastery. I was alone, and I sat in the stillness, in which the only sound was the rushing of the waterfall. As I watched, I became aware of the continuity I could see between the changes in the flow of the water and the variations in the sound. Soon, the continuity between the flow and the sound of the water appeared to be constant and unchanging.

Suddenly, my mind leaped to a new perspective. I realized that the sound and the flow of the water were not constant, but endlessly changing. My mind leaped again and I realized that my thoughts, as well as the ideas and theories I had been grasping, were also changing and impermanent. I reflected that without this sudden burst of spaciousness, I would have been in the midst of studying the Dharma and missed the very essence of its teaching.

Opening techniques that cultivate spaciousness are quite easy for most people to learn, once they have practiced attending and concentrating. When you start to practice opening, you should continue to practice attending and concentrating in some of your extended sessions. Do only one technique during each extended session. We recommend that you divide your extended sessions equally among the three techniques: attending, concentrating, and opening. For example, if you are doing three thirty minute sessions per week, like Maria, then you would do one session per week each of attending, concentrating, and opening.

Opening techniques involve disengaging from our usual way of experiencing reality. This is a lot simpler to do than it sounds. We introduce two types of basic opening techniques: one involves remembering a time when you experienced a sense of space or vastness, the other involves paying attention in a particular manner to the sensations of breathing.

BRIAN'S FIRST EXPERIENCE WITH OPENING

Brian is beginning his morning meditation session. He is starting to practice opening today; on the advice of his teacher, he has gotten up a little earlier. *Opening techniques tend to change your state of consciousness in a more powerful way than the other practices. You should allow enough time to make the shift in your state of consciousness and then return to your usual one before the end of the session. Fifteen minutes is not really enough time to do that; a better minimum is twenty minutes.*

Brian is now used to waking early and he enjoys his meditation sessions, so getting up five minutes earlier is acceptable. He sits down on the pillow in his living room and focuses his intention for the session. He remembers his goals, and thinks briefly about the purpose of this session: experiencing a sense of mental vastness and a "letting go." He notices that he feels a little tense, especially in his shoulders and neck. *If you feel tense, spend a little time getting relaxed so that you will be better able to perform the technique. Centering is a good way to get the mind and body into a calm state in which you can start the other practices.* Brian centers on the sensations in his lower abdomen for a couple of minutes. As he feels the warmth in his lower abdomen, he relaxes, and senses the muscles in his shoulders and neck loosen.

Brian feels ready to do the opening technique. He remembers times when he was in a place where he felt a sense of vastness, of space all around him. One memory is of being on a mountaintop; another is of being at the seashore, looking out over the ocean. In both experiences, he was alone, and he remembers the sense of being able to see forever. As he becomes more aware of these memories, the one of the mountaintop seems to possess a greater feeling of vastness. Brian focuses on that, and the memory of the seashore fades.

Brian concentrates on those details of the mountaintop experience that give him the sense of vastness. He notices the feel of the air, the blue of the sky, the ground falling away beneath him, and the expanse of land stretching out to the horizon in all directions. As he focuses on these details, he suddenly has the sense that he is not remembering accurately. His body seems much larger in the memory than it should be. He feels a little jolt of surprise as he realizes this. The memory vanishes suddenly, and he is back, sitting on his pillow with his eyes closed. He remembers that his teacher said, *When we do the opening techniques, a sign of success is a change in how we perceive our bodies. Spaciousness occurs when we let go of how we usually experience our selves, which allows a different experience to move in. If this new experience seems unusual, our mind may be a little startled and return to the experience we are used to. Just accept this, realize that the technique was successful, and repeat it.*

Brian is pleased with himself. It was rather exciting to experience himself as a huge being on top of the mountain. He refocuses his mind on the memory of the mountaintop. He tries to remember how it felt to experience himself as huge, but his mind does not seem to want to cooperate. He notices the details of the mountaintop, but his perception of his body does not change, and he starts to get frustrated. *When you experience a sensory alteration while practicing opening, there is a temptation to try to evoke the same altered sensations when you repeat the practice. It is a mistake to do so. In practicing the opening technique, you must let go of trying to evoke any particular change. When your mind experiences spaciousness, the changes will come and you should just experience them.*

Brian remembers this advice, and realizes that he needs to refocus on the sense of vastness. That in itself is enjoyable, even without the sensory changes. He remembers how peaceful it was to look out from the mountaintop and see the land stretching away beneath him. Everything seemed so far away. He was aware of the sights below him, but they were all at a distance and he could encompass them all in his vision. As Brian becomes absorbed in this experience of vastness, he suddenly realizes that he does not know where he is. He has a moment of complete uncertainty, and then feels as if he is floating above the mountaintop and moving higher into the sky. As he starts to think about this, the sensation fades and he is back to his awareness of remembering the mountaintop while he sits on a pillow in his living room. *The experience of not knowing where you are, the uncertainty, is a sign of spaciousness. In that spaciousness, your mind is not grasping onto anything, it has let go. When it has opened like that, it can then create an experience that may be quite different from your usual way of experiencing things.*

Brian feels a little tired, and finds himself just centering on the sensations in his lower abdomen. He hears his alarm beep at him, and is surprised to find the session over already. He reflects on the sense of vastness that he experienced, and also the change in his time perception. He then brings his awareness back to his whole body, reorients himself to time and place, and opens his eyes.

MARIA'S FIRST EXPERIENCE WITH OPENING

Maria sits down for her first session of opening. She focuses her intention, remembering her goals for meditation and for this session, and closes her eyes. Maria centers her awareness on the sensations of air moving in and out of her nose. She attends to thoughts and sensations as they arise, identifying and disengaging from them. After a couple of minutes, she feels her mind and body settle into a comfortable, relaxed state. Now that she is relaxed, she is ready to practice the opening technique.

Maria brings her attention to the sensations of movement in her chest as she breathes. She notices how her chest expands as she breathes in, and contracts as she breathes out. She observes how the movement occurs to the back and sides as well as to the front. She focuses her attention more and more on the movement of her chest and less on the movement of the air. As Maria becomes more aware of the expansion and contraction of her chest, she also starts to notice some movement in her abdomen and shoulders. She notices that her abdomen expands as she breathes in, and it contracts as she breathes out. She becomes aware that her shoulders lift slightly as she inhales and fall slightly as she exhales. Maria observes how the movements in her shoulders, chest, and abdomen all coincide. She focuses even more on the movement in her shoulders, chest, and abdomen, observing how the expansion occurs in all directions (up, down, back, front, and sides); and then observes how the contraction occurs in all those directions as well.

Maria then begins to imagine that other parts of her body are also expanding and contracting. As she focuses on the expansion in her chest and the lift of her shoulders, she imagines that her neck and upper arms are expanding. She then feels as if her neck and upper arms contract as her shoulders fall and her chest contracts. Then, as she feels her abdomen expand and contract, she imagines that her pelvic and hip area expands and contracts. Maria then allows the imagined sensations of expansion and contraction to move outward to her arms, hands, and legs.

She suddenly has the thought, "This is ridiculous. Your hands and feet can't be expanding and contracting!" She remembers, *When you practice opening, you will be letting go of your usual way of experiencing things. This means that you will be experiencing things that "can't happen." Just enjoy that, and keep going along with your experience. Pretend that the changes are actually occurring.* Maria goes back to sensing the expansion and contraction in her chest, shoulders, and abdomen. After a few breaths, she imagines the expansion and contraction moving outward again, and soon feels as if her arms and legs are expanding and contracting as well.

Maria is feeling very quiet and peaceful. Soon, she realizes that she has lost track of the size and shape of her body. Her body perception is varying; she feels like a round ball, and then like an oval. She feels like she has become very large and then feels as if she is very small. Her thoughts seem to be at a great distance. They are quiet, lost in a sense of interior vastness. Even her sense of having a body begins to fade. Concepts of size and shape no longer seem to apply. Images come and go, but she does not notice them. She is just aware of a deep sense of peace and quiet, and feels like her awareness is floating in a sea of comfort.

Maria hears her watch alarm go off as if from a great distance. She reflects on how much her perceptions changed during this session. She also reflects on how varied her experience during opening meditation has been. *It is normal to have a lot of variation in your experience when you practice opening. Some days nothing seems to happen, other days you have a lot of imagery, and on others you have a radically altered experience of your body. Just accept the experience your mind gives you, and realize that any change in your perception was the result of an experience of spaciousness to some degree.* Maria feels a sense of gratitude for the experience. She then brings her attention to her whole body, wiggling her fingers and toes to restore her sense of her body's usual boundaries (she finds that this takes a minute or so). She then remembers the day and time and her surroundings, gradually bringing her mind back to her current situation. After another minute, she opens her eyes.

Maria still feels a little spaced-out, and fumbles a bit as she gets up from her session. She is a little unsteady as she walks, as though she were not quite aware of where the floor is. *When you experience a deep sense of spaciousness, you may feel like you are not quite back to your usual reality after your meditation. If that is the case, have a light snack and that will bring you back into your body.* Maria goes into the kitchen and fixes herself a piece of toast. As she eats it, she feels that she is reorienting fully to her surroundings.

THE BASICS OF OPENING

Opening involves allowing your mind to experience a sense of vastness or spaciousness. When your mind becomes spacious, your usual way of perceiving reality can change.

People have varied responses to the different opening techniques, especially at first. We describe two techniques in the instructions; pick one that sounds good to you, and if it doesn't work, try the other one.

Notice that the opening techniques used by Brian and Maria required some skill in concentrating and attending. Brian started by concentrating on an image, and then focusing on a particular aspect of the image, the vastness. Maria started by centering on sensations, and then concentrating on a particular imagined sensory experience. Both of them used attending to identify and disengage from distracting thoughts.

The experience of spaciousness occurs when your mind lets go of its usual way of organizing reality. Your mind then has the opportunity to reorganize reality in a different manner. When this happens, your perceptions change. The changes in your perceptions are the *result* of the experience of spaciousness—they are not the actual experience. That is why the particular changes are not important. If your perceptions change, then your mind has experienced spaciousness prior to the change, and that is what matters.

Perceiving things differently enhances your ability to be a fun and creative person. As you get better at opening, your spaciousness will increase, and you will find yourself spontaneously coming up with creative and humorous ideas.

INSTRUCTIONS FOR EXTENDED OPENING TECHNIQUE 1 (BRIAN'S)

1. Sit in a comfortable place. You will want to stay warm during the practice. Also, make sure that you are not likely to be disturbed, as distractions can be jarring.

2. Focus your intention by thinking of your long-range goals for meditation, and your immediate goal for the session. Your immediate goal for an opening session is to allow your mind to experience a change in your perceptions.
3. Practice a centering or attending technique until you feel relaxed. This should take only a couple of minutes.
4. Remember a time when you were in a place where you felt a sense of vastness. A few places that people commonly recall are the ocean, the seashore, scuba diving, mountaintops, deserts, and being under the night sky. Focus your attention on the sense of vastness, of space all around you. As you experience that sense of space, pretend that sounds, sights, and other sensations are moving farther and farther away. You can observe them, but they are at a great distance.
5. If your mind gets distracted by other phenomena, identify them and let them go. Return your awareness to the sense of vastness; it can help to imagine that the distractions are moving farther and farther away. As you do this, you will find that you begin to feel changes in your perception of your body and in other elements of the image.
6. You may feel yourself moving upward, or shrinking, or expanding. Continue to keep your mind on the experience of vastness and accept these changes in your perception. As you do this, you may find that the original image fades and you start having other images come, or even move into a dream state. Just continue to identify these and disengage from them. If your mind gets caught by them, then go back to the original image and your experience of vastness.

7. At the end of the session, reflect on your experience, and then gradually reorient yourself to your body and the time and place before you open your eyes.

INSTRUCTIONS FOR EXTENDED OPENING TECHNIQUE 2 (MARIA'S)

1. Sit in a comfortable place, set your intention, and relax (as described in steps 1–3 of technique 1).
2. Focus on the expansion and contraction of your chest as you breathe in and out. Notice how your chest naturally expands as you inhale and then contracts as you exhale. Focus your attention less on the movement of air, and more on the expansion and contraction.
3. As you feel more aware of the movement in your chest, extend your awareness to your abdomen. Notice that it is expanding along with your chest as you breathe in, and contracting as you breathe out. The movement may be slight, it may also vary. Just experience it as it is.
4. Now imagine that the expansion and contraction are moving outward from your chest and abdomen into your shoulders, hips, arms, legs, and head. Pretend that your whole body is expanding and contracting gently as you breathe.
5. If you get distracted, just identify the distraction, disengage from it, and go back to focusing on the sense of expansion and contraction. If you lose track of the experience of your whole body expanding and contracting, go back to being aware of your chest and abdomen expanding and contracting.

6. As you do this, you may have a sense that your body is changing position, shape, or size. When this happens, you are experiencing spaciousness. Avoid analyzing the body perceptions and simply observe them, focusing on the sense of space inside you.
7. If thoughts or images go by, just observe them without trying to analyze them. Make note of them, and if you get caught up in them just go back to being aware of expansion and contraction.
8. At the end of the session, reflect on your experience. Spaciousness comes from letting go of your usual way of experiencing your body and allowing your mind to experience it differently. Make note of any images or thoughts that seemed particularly important. Then, gradually reorient to your whole body and the time and place before you open your eyes.

BRIEF OPENING PRACTICE

Like the other practices, opening has a brief version. The extended technique causes you to experience spaciousness in a way that radically changes your state of consciousness. You cannot do this while involved in your other daily activities. In order to access spaciousness during the day, you need a brief opening technique that will not disorient you.

Accessing spaciousness during the day is critically important for people who feel pressure from having too many things to do. That includes most of us, most of the time, as the pace of life seems to accelerate. We often feel crowded by the many things that demand our immediate attention. Accessing spaciousness frequently during the day can give relief from that feeling of pressure—though the demands will still be there, we will not feel them crowding in on us. Then we can deal with them more efficiently.

The brief technique requires you to remember a sense of space or vastness. If you have experienced space or vastness in the extended sessions, you should remember that. Then you take a deep breath in, pretending that there is space inside your entire body and that the air is filling it. Then you release the breath, imagining that all the space is surrounding you, and that all the things demanding your attention are moving into the distance.

Brian's Experience with Brief Opening Practice

Brian is sitting at his desk, working on a presentation he must make in a couple of hours. He is feeling some pressure about this, but feels sure that he will be ready in time. Then the phone rings. The caller informs him of a problem that needs his attention. As he hangs up the phone, a coworker comes to his desk and hands him a memo marked "urgent." Brian immediately feels his tension level leap upward. His shoulders and jaw tense, his stomach tightens, his thoughts are angry and unprintable. It seems like everything is demanding his attention at once. He feels frustrated and angry.

Brian remembers the brief spaciousness exercise he has worked on for a few days. Space is exactly what he needs right now. He focuses his intention to experience a sense of space and then takes a deep breath. As he does so, he imagines that his whole body is expanding; that the air is filling him like a balloon. He then releases the breath, and imagines that everything around him is moving farther away.

Suddenly, everything seems to calm down. Time seems frozen. Brian realizes that he is still holding the memo he was handed.

Brian takes another deep breath, imagining his body expanding and then releases it, imagining things moving farther away. Now he feels that he has some breathing room. He thinks about the big picture. He has the presentation, the phone call, and the memo to deal with. As his mind scans these three tasks, he is able to prioritize intelligently. He really has only a little more work to do on his presentation. There are a couple of people he can call to deal with the matter raised in the memo, and he can then take care of the problem he was informed of in the phone call. Brian feels reasonably comfortable. He has a lot to do in a short time, but he does not feel overwhelmed.

Maria's Experience with Brief Opening Practice

Maria has picked up her children from day-care after a stressful day at work. Her children are irritable and quarreling with each other. When she gets home, she finds a bunch of bills in the mailbox. As she urges her complaining children into the house, the phone rings. She rushes to get the phone, dropping the mail all over the floor. Her husband is calling to let her know that he will be delayed at work, and won't be able to take care of the errands that she had asked him to run. Just then, her older child pushes the younger one onto the floor, who then proceeds to wail, "Mommy! She pushed me down!"

Maria feels like she is ready to explode—everything is just too much for her. As she takes a deep breath to yell at her children, she suddenly remembers the brief spaciousness technique. She imagines the breath filling her body. Her body seems to grow much bigger in response, which feels good. She releases the breath without yelling, but imagines that she is blowing the things around her away from her. That feels better. Maria repeats this during her next breath, and she feels like she is standing taller and straighter.

Maria now has the understanding that things will be all right. She doesn't have to take care of everything in the next two seconds. She hears her husband's voice over the phone, "Honey, are you OK?" She laughs and responds, "Well, it's a little crazy here right now, but we're all right. I've got to run and deal with the kids. Love you, bye."

INSTRUCTIONS FOR BRIEF OPENING PRACTICE

1. Focus your intention to experience a sense of increased space within and around you.
2. Inhale, and imagine that you are breathing in space as you inhale—that your whole body is expanding, and that the air is filling your whole body all the way out to your fingers and toes. (You need not close your eyes.)
3. As you exhale, imagine that you are breathing out space, and that this creates a great distance between you and everything else around you.
4. The inhalation and exhalation should be easy and free. There is no need to strain to breathe deeply.
5. The image of space within and without should come easily. Avoid straining to make it work.
6. Repeat this for one or at most two more breaths, and then reflect on your experience.

Brian's Results from Opening

Brian has practiced the extended opening technique nine times over the past month. He interspersed his sessions of practicing opening with sessions in which he practiced attending and concentrating. His experience with opening has been somewhat varied. In the beginning, he found himself trying to recreate his first experience. This was frustrating, as the more he tried to create the sensations of floating upward, the more stuck that he felt. His teacher advised him, *The perceptual changes during opening occur when our mind lets go of its usual way of organizing the world. When that happens, our perceptions change. That change is going to be rather random, so it will not be the same change every time. If the desire to experience a particular change arises, identify it, disengage from it, and go back to experiencing the sense of vastness.*

Brian found the advice helpful, and he could relate it to his difficulty with attending. He could see how practicing attending and getting better at letting go of distractions would also help him with opening. Once Brian accepted the fact that his experience would be varied, he found the opening practice to be very enjoyable. It became like taking a little vacation, without having to leave town.

Brian finds the brief opening practice quite helpful. He is able to snap out of his automatic response to stressful situations when he can gain a sense of space around him. This is especially helpful when he is trying to keep his temper at home. When things upset him, he usually feels as if his focus is narrowing, like he is having tunnel vision. The brief practice seems to change this. His visual field opens up, and his shoulders and chest relax; this changes his emotional response to one that is calmer and more reasonable. *Opening creates room for responses that are different from your usual ones. This is why the brief practice is so important. When your temper is starting to get the best of you, opening enables you to see the situation differently. Then there is no need to lose your temper.*

Maria's Results from Opening

Maria has practiced the extended opening technique five times over the past month. She practiced concentrating and attending during the other seven extended practice sessions. Her initial experience with opening was so interesting and pleasant that she wanted to practice only that. *Opening can lead to very interesting and fun experiences, but you need to develop the other mental qualities to balance your mind. This means that you must spend some sessions practicing attending and some sessions practicing concentrating, and not just practice opening.*

By interspersing the other practices with the opening sessions, Maria finds the other practices more enjoyable. She still finds the concentrating sessions to be rather difficult, but the opening sessions seem to give her a rest and she is able to continue to make progress in concentrating. Several times during opening practice, she experienced images that were unclear and, try as she might, she was unable to make them out. *Remember, the opening practice is to help you experience spaciousness. You experience the spaciousness when your mind lets go of how it is organizing your perceptions. That occurs before the new images become clear. When the new images become clear, your mind is no longer using the spaciousness. It is using the other mental qualities to reorganize its perceptions. As you practice concentrating and increase your clarity and steadiness, the new images will become clearer.* Maria feels that the opening sessions are the most enjoyable of all the practice sessions. They give her a sense of rest and ease that sometimes lasts for hours after the practice.

Maria finds the brief practice useful. She has been practicing it a few times per day, and experiences a brief sense of peace when she does it. She has also used it during meetings, and finds that she does not get nearly as flustered. In meetings, when she is getting ready to speak, she often has a sense of shrinking—as if the stares of the other people were compressing her. When she does the brief practice just before speaking, her perception changes and she feels a sense of expansion, as if she were large, and the attention of the others remains at a comfortable distance.

Maria has also played around with the opening technique for relaxation. She starts with the experience of expansion and contraction in her chest and abdomen. Then, instead of allowing that sense to expand and spread over her whole body, she focuses the experience of expansion and contraction into specific areas of her body that feel tense. This causes a sense of letting go and space in that area. Maria has found that if she does a brief mental scan of her body before she eats lunch, and uses the opening technique to relax areas that are tense, then she feels much more relaxed while eating. Her stomach feels much more comfortable, and she does not have difficulties with indigestion.

Both Brian and Maria are having success with opening practice. However, they both feel that something is missing. The experiences during opening are enjoyable and restful, yet they seem to lack direction. They were worried about this and asked their teacher. The response was, *You are right to be getting a little bored. Just practicing opening and experiencing spaciousness and then some imagery can get to be like using a drug. The experience may be fun, but it is not developing your mind. Once you are having success with opening practice, then you need to start using it in the applications. It is a powerful technique that will help you move toward your goals for meditation when you apply it correctly. It also must be used in conjunction with the other techniques, attending and concentrating.*

CONCLUSION

Opening consists of focusing attention on a sense of vastness or space in a way that allows you to let go of the way you usually perceive the world. When you let go of your usual way of perceiving the world, you are using the mental quality of spaciousness. This spaciousness is often experienced as a sense of vastness within yourself.

After you let go, your mind will often reorganize your perceptions into a different experience. This can manifest as imagery, or changes in your position or body size. Just accept these experiences as they arise, and keep letting go of them. Soon, you will learn how to use these experiences to help you move toward your goals. For now, just let them go.

Do not practice opening every day. Balance opening with sessions of attending or concentrating. As you practice concentrating and attending, you will increase your ability to work with and use the images and other experiences that arise during opening.

Opening practice usually takes longer than fifteen minutes to complete comfortably. Generally, an opening session should be at least twenty minutes long. That gives you enough time to get into the experience of spaciousness, enjoy it, and return to your usual way of experiencing the world.

You are having success with opening when you have some change in your perception. This change may occur with visual or auditory imagery, or it may be in your kinesthetic sense, a feeling that you are moving or changing size.

Remember that the sense of spaciousness occurs before these changes in perception. This means that you must not try to achieve the same changes from session to session. Trying to experience a specific change in perception will impede the experience of opening. Just focus on the experience of vastness, or expansion and contraction, and then accept what happens.

The brief opening practice is helpful for bringing the effects of spaciousness into your daily life. It can be most useful for helping you deal with situations in which you feel very nervous or angry. It allows you to step back from a situation and gain a broader perspective.

TIPS

Remember to focus your intention at the beginning of each session. This is especially important for opening practice, as your mind tends to drift when you are experiencing spaciousness. Focusing your intention will help it to drift in constructive directions.

If you are having difficulty with distractions, identify them and disengage from them. Keep coming back to either the sensation of expansion and contraction, or the sense of vastness.

You can work with either or both of the techniques described. Play with them, and use whichever one works best for you. You may find that one works well one day, and the other works well another day.

SIX

summary of the four practices: where you should be now

Perseverance is the supreme virtue, for when you cultivate it, you will surely succeed.

An Ornament to the Sutras

In the preceding four chapters, we introduced you to a series of techniques from the four meditative practices of centering, attending, concentrating, and opening. The techniques that you have learned have developed your mental qualities of steadiness, pliancy, warmth, clarity, and spaciousness. It usually takes students between two and four months to reach this point. Before we move on to the applications in part II, we summarize the practices, the techniques, and the results that you should be experiencing.

Please remember the brief techniques for each practice in addition to the extended techniques; the brief techniques are critically important. You should spend at least ninety minutes per week with the extended techniques. If you also practice the brief techniques, then you will make rapid progress even with such a small investment of time.

Summaries of the brief and extended techniques for each meditative practice follow.

CENTERING

Definition—Maintaining continuous awareness of a physical or mental object. The object you maintain awareness of is called your center.

Purpose—Develops mental steadiness and prepares you to do the more advanced techniques of attending and concentrating.

Extended Technique—Focus on the sensations in your lower abdomen. If you get distracted, return your awareness to those sensations.

Brief Technique—Focus on a simple mental phrase such as "calm—relaxed" or "calm—alert" for up to thirty seconds.

Success—You are ready to move on when you can maintain awareness of the sensations in your lower abdomen for thirty seconds without being distracted. (For most people, thirty seconds is about equal to five breaths.)

Simple Application—Center on the mental phrase "calm—relaxed" for several minutes as you fall asleep

Continued Practice—You need not practice the extended centering technique once you move to attending. Continue to practice the brief technique several times per day for stress reduction.

ATTENDING

Definition—Identifying and disengaging from sensations, thoughts, and emotions.

Purpose—Develops mental pliancy and warmth.

Extended Technique—Focus on the sensations of air moving at the entrance of your nostrils. Identify and disengage from any distractions.

Brief Technique—Observe the sensations, thoughts, and feelings that are going through your mind. Spend only ten to twenty seconds recalling your experience of the preceding couple of minutes.

Success—You are able to perform the extended technique for fifteen minutes without feeling strained.

Simple Application—Center on different parts of your body in a progressive sequence. Identify and disengage from the sensations in each part before you move on to the next one. (This can be extremely relaxing.)

Continued Practice—As you move on to concentrating, you should practice the extended attending technique for one-third of your extended practice sessions. You should practice the brief technique several times per day, three days per week.

CONCENTRATING

Definition—Maintaining intense awareness of a mental object and perceiving it in complete detail without being distracted.

Purpose—Develops mental steadiness and clarity.

Extended Technique—Concentrate on the memory of a simple shape, a simple sound, or a simple movement.

Brief Technique—Concentrate for one to two minutes on the memory of an event that occurred earlier in the day.

Success—You are able to hold the mental image steady and perceive its details for ten seconds.

Continued Practice—After moving on to opening, practice the extended concentrating technique for one-third of your extended practice sessions. You should practice the brief technique two or three times per day, four days per week.

OPENING

Definition—Letting go of how the mind organizes perceptions, so that a different perspective can arise.

Purpose—Develops mental spaciousness.

Extended Technique 1 – Imagine being in a wide-open place, such as on a mountaintop. Imagine that everything is very far away and feel your mind filling the vastness.

Extended Technique 2—Feel your chest and abdomen expand as you inhale and contract as you exhale. Imagine that your whole body is expanding and contracting as you breathe in and out.

Brief Technique—Take a deep breath and imagine it filling your whole body with space. As you breathe out, imagine that the space is surrounding you and everything else is moving farther away.

Success—You experience a change in body awareness, position sense, or a change in the sense of how time passes.

Continued Practice—Until you start practicing the applications, do the extended opening technique in one-third of your extended sessions. Practice the brief technique several times every day.

HOW YOU SHOULD PROGRESS

If you are spending the minimum amount of time practicing the extended sessions (ninety minutes per week), and you are practicing the brief techniques regularly, then it should take you about four months to complete all four practices. The usual progression is shown below.

Weeks 1 and 2—Practice the extended centering technique ninety minutes per week. Practice the brief centering technique several times per day.

Weeks 3 through 7—Practice the extended attending technique ninety minutes per week. You need not practice the extended centering technique. Continue to practice the brief centering technique three to four times per day. Practice the brief attending technique five to six times per day.

Weeks 8 through 14—Practice the extended concentrating technique sixty minutes per week. Practice the extended attending technique thirty minutes per week. Continue to practice the brief centering technique three to four times per day. Practice the brief attending technique five to six times per day, three days per week, and practice the brief concentrating technique two to three times per day, four days per week.

Weeks 15 through 18—Practice the extended opening technique thirty minutes per week, and practice the extended attending and concentrating techniques thirty minutes per week each, as well. Continue to practice the brief attending technique several times per day, three days per week. Practice the brief concentrating technique two or three times per day, four days per week, and the brief opening technique several times every day.

BRIAN'S RESULTS SO FAR

It has been almost five months since Brian had the talk with his sister, Karen, in which she advised him to meditate. He has taken her advice, and has been practicing consistently for the past four months. During a family get-together, the two of them have some time to talk.

Karen says, "We haven't talked in a while. How are you doing? You seem better than you did five months ago."

Brian replies, "I am better. I'm a lot more hopeful."

"That's good. Do you mind telling me what's changed?"

Brian smiles self-consciously, "Well, I took your advice."

"Really!" jokes his sister.

"Yes, I actually started meditating four months ago. It has been a big help."

"I'm glad to hear that. What changes have you noticed?" Karen asks.

"Hmm ... for one thing, I feel more relaxed. The pressure at work hasn't changed, but I don't feel as exhausted by it. I also seem to get more rest on my days off."

"So, the meditation is helping you relax?"

"It's more than that. I feel less irritable, I don't get angry as easily. I feel like I can see things from someone else's point of view, not just my own."

"That sounds good—anything else?"

Brian reflects, "I seem to be more accepting of change. If something goes wrong and I have to change plans, I don't feel as upset, I can change my plans constructively. Here's an example: One day, my son and I were supposed to go to a ball game. Unfortunately, the car broke down two blocks away. Ordinarily, I would have been completely upset and lost my temper. Instead, I took a deep breath. Though I was disappointed, I stayed calm. After getting the car towed to the shop, my son and I decided to go to the park and throw a ball around ourselves. Then we went and had ice cream together. It turned out to be a great day for the two of us."

"Brian, that's fantastic!"

"You know, its not so much that things have changed. It's me that's changed. My mind is working better for me. I remember things better and I have more creative ideas. I have more influence over my moods and reactions. I have a lot more hope and peace than I used to. I don't feel stuck any more."

"So are you going to continue practicing?"

"You bet. I'm comfortable with the basic techniques now, and will be starting the applications. After seeing so much benefit from just the basics, I'm looking forward to experiencing what I can achieve with the applications."

MARIA'S RESULTS SO FAR

It has been five months since Maria and Susan had their talk about the possibility of Maria trying meditation. Since that time, they have talked only briefly, but they had arranged to meet again for lunch today so they could have some time together.

After they had chatted over lunch for a while, Susan commented, "You seem to be more relaxed than you were a few months ago. Are you feeling better?"

Maria smiled. "I am, thank you. I have to admit that your suggestion that I practice meditation was a lifesaver."

"Well I'm glad to hear that. You're very welcome. So you must have gotten over your fears about meditation being too Eastern."

"Yes, it doesn't feel strange at all," Maria replied. "The techniques make sense and I'm certainly not practicing a different religion."

"What about the time commitment?"

"That took some getting used to at first, but I was able to find ways to fit it into my day. My husband, Kevin, was a little reluctant, but he is seeing so much positive change in me that now he is happy to give me the time."

"Are you using the brief techniques?"

"The brief techniques are so helpful. I am surprised at how much benefit I get from doing those short exercises. Without them, I don't think I would have made the progress I did."

"What did you find most helpful?"

Maria laughed. "You know, I used to think that I was mentally ill because of the way I would get scattered, frustrated, and irritable when I was stressed. Just hearing that it might be an imbalance in my mental qualities that could be corrected by simple exercises was such a relief."

"Yes, that is comforting."

"And now I am so different," Maria continued. "I can't believe how much more coherent I feel. I used to get scattered so easily. Now I can stay focused, prioritize, and deal with things. I still get emotional, but I can keep my feelings from exploding out of me."

"It sounds like you have made some big changes."

"I'm definitely more peaceful. You know, one day my deadline on a project had been moved up. So instead of being ahead, I was behind. I stayed late at work and you can imagine how stressed I felt. When I got home, Kevin was irritable, the sink had backed up, the kids were fighting. I was starting to get the old feeling of running on a treadmill. Ordinarily I would have tried to fix everything at once, gotten completely overwhelmed, then become irritable and developed a headache. Instead, I took a deep breath and told everyone that I needed absolute silence for five minutes. That surprised them so much that I actually got three minutes! During that three minutes, I was able to become calm and alert. I was able to disengage from the thoughts about work because I couldn't do anything about work at the time. At the end of the three minutes, the kids started complaining. I told Bill that he would be responsible for dealing with the sink. I would take the kids and we would stay out of his hair for the next couple of hours. I thought the kids would be a challenge, but we went in to the living room and tickled each other for the next half hour. Then I read them stories for a while. After that, the kids had calmed down enough to go and play by themselves. Bill had been able to fix the sink during that time, and he was feeling good. We actually got to sit together quietly for a little while before we had to start the dinner routine. It was such a different outcome from what usually would have happened."

"Much more enjoyable, I imagine," Susan nodded.

"That's right. And these changes are just happening. I simply focus on my goals and do the exercises, and my life is straightening out. Instead of life being stressful, its just challenging. I'm becoming a better person. That is what makes me excited about starting the applications."

PART TWO

IMPROVING YOUR HEALTH, PERFORMANCE, RELATIONSHIPS, & SPIRITUALITY

seven

introduction to the four applications

By now, you have developed your mental qualities, and gained enough familiarity with the basic practices to start applying them. You know that centering involves maintaining continuous awareness of something; you have experienced how to identify things and disengage from them while attending; you know the intense focus on details that concentrating gives you. Finally, you have felt the changes in perception that accompany opening.

The effort that you have expended so far has prepared you to apply the basic meditation practices directly to your goals. You have already discovered benefits that come from simply strengthening and balancing your five mental qualities. Now you will use your enhanced mental abilities to move more directly toward your goals.

The principles that you have used to succeed with the basic techniques are also required for success with the applications. You will learn both extended and brief techniques, and you will perform each of the three phases—intention, execution, and reflection—during each of the application techniques.

In addition to practicing the application techniques, you should also spend a little time continuing to work on the basics. The applications also develop the five mental qualities, but simultaneously keeping up with the basics will be better than just practicing the applications. It is like being a gymnast, and spending some time focusing on stretching exercises. Those are basic, but spending some time stretching improves the gymnast's flexibility more than just practicing the routines for competition would.

We recommend that you spend one-third of your extended sessions practicing a basic technique. If you are doing three extended sessions per week, then you would spend one of those sessions doing a basic technique. You should rotate through the extended attending, concentrating, and opening techniques in turn. So, if you were doing one basic extended session per week, then you would do the basic attending technique the first week, the basic concentrating technique the second week, and the basic opening technique the third week, and then repeat the sequence.

In part II, we describe applications of meditation that will improve your health, your performance, your relationships, and your spirituality—in that order. We organized the material in this way because the applications become more complex as you proceed. Unlike part I, however, you need not work with the techniques from one chapter before you go on to the next. Each chapter contains three techniques, and within each chapter you should practice the techniques in order, as each builds on the previous one. But any order of the four applications is possible.

eight

Health: strengthening the mind–body connection

The Mind is like the rider and the body is like the horse. [In other words, your mind can, like a rider directing a horse, learn to direct the body.]

A famous Buddhist saying

The mind and the body are intimately connected, and constantly influence each other. For those of you who might doubt this, perform the following "thought experiment." Mentally scan your body, and assess how relaxed or tense you are. Now, imagine that you are looking over your mail for the day. As you sort through the envelopes, you come across an official-looking envelope from the IRS. As you imagine this, what happens in your body? Now, imagine that you open the envelope and find a letter stating that there was a mistake on your tax return, and you overpaid by $100; accompanying the letter is a check for that amount. Now what happens to your body?

Since your mind and body are connected, meditation can help you strengthen that connection and influence it in a positive way. As your mind–body connection becomes stronger and more positive, you will experience a sense of physical peace. You will move more efficiently, your breathing and heartbeat will be calmer, and you will feel more inner harmony. By applying the meditative practices of centering, attending, concentrating, and opening, your mind will have a powerful, positive effect on your body.

We recommend that you practice these health applications even if you are not "sick." Being healthy is different from not being sick. You don't need to wait for something to go wrong before you work on improving your health. After all, you don't wait for your car engine to burn up before you change its oil. Why should you wait for your body to burn out before you start to take care of it? The exercises you will learn are excellent for improving your state of health. But before we introduce the three health applications in this chapter, we need to make a couple of points.

The first point is that meditation should not be used as a cure-all. We emphasize this because we have met people who believed that using meditation meant that they should not use other forms of medical treatment. There is absolutely no reason not to do both. Meditation is not meant to replace medicine. In fact, trying to treat a serious medical condition with meditation alone is dangerous. If you are receiving treatment from a physician, you can continue to receive that treatment and still use the exercises that we describe. If you are having symptoms, then we urge you to speak with a physician about them and not try to treat them with meditation alone. Meditation can certainly augment standard medical treatments, but it should never be used as a substitute for medical treatment.

People with mental disorders can be especially prone to thinking that meditation alone will cure them. However, since meditation exercises the mind, people with mental disorders can also feel strained from the effects of meditation. Those people need to realize that professional mental health treatment and even medications are likely to be helpful. Medicine and therapy can augment the benefits of meditation.

The second point is that if you do get sick, it is not necessarily your own fault. We believe that a lot of damage is done when people are told that they have caused their own illnesses. There are a lot of random factors involved in illness. Some people who smoke live to be ninety, and others get lung cancer and die at fifty. There are people with type A behavior who will never have a heart attack. There are wonderfully spiritual people who nevertheless will die young. Our minds like to find reasons for things, but blaming people for having an illness can be abusive and even ridiculous. Does a baby born with AIDS cause their disease? Is a child with fetal alcohol syndrome responsible for their mother's alcoholism?

Meditation should be used to help you find peace. If you are ill, you should not blame yourself for causing your illness. Your illness has many causes. You should take responsibility for your mental and physical behavior: many times, behavior and emotions have a negative influence on health. Your task is to look at your life and work on improving yourself. Meditation gives you the ability to do that in a powerful way. But even should you become spiritually perfect, your body is simply not going to last forever. Of course, if you are spiritually developed, that won't matter as much to you. Holy people don't seem to mind the fact of their own death nearly as much as the people who grieve for them.

We introduce three health applications in this chapter. The first, autonomic relaxation, uses centering and attending skills to evoke a deep state of relaxation. The second, inner harmony, uses attending and concentrating skills to create a more positive relationship between you and your body. The third, inner light, uses attending, concentrating, and opening skills to bring healing energy into your body.

AUTONOMIC RELAXATION

Physicians divide the nervous system into two general parts or subsystems. The voluntary nervous system is the one that is under your conscious control. Right now, you are using it to turn the pages of this book. You use your voluntary nervous system to interact in a deliberate way with your environment.

The other part of your nervous system is the autonomic, or involuntary, nervous system. It is the subsystem that you do not control consciously, unless you have practiced techniques like the ones you are about to learn. The autonomic nervous system controls your resting muscle tension, your skin temperature, your heart rate, your breathing (most of the time), and the activity of your digestive tract. It also regulates your immune system, your hormone production, and many other physical processes. Right now, your autonomic nervous system is making sure that your heart and lungs work properly while you concentrate on these words. Your autonomic nervous system is a vital regulator of your body's functions.

When people think of relaxation, they think of reducing their muscle tension, which is only one function of the autonomic nervous system. Autonomic relaxation relaxes five parts of the autonomic nervous system, bestowing a deeper and more thorough experience of relaxation. The instructions that we give are similar to those given in numerous books as "autogenic exercises," but our instructions contain some important differences.

Brian's Experience with Autonomic Relaxation

Brian has already seen some health benefits from practicing the basic techniques, but he wants more results. He decides to practice some meditation techniques for improving his health. Brian starts with autonomic relaxation. He wanted to start with a more advanced exercise, but his teacher said, *The first health application is autonomic relaxation. It will produce a deeply relaxed state that increases the body's self-healing abilities. Autonomic relaxation is also a stepping-stone to more advanced techniques.*

As Brian sits down for his morning session, he feels a little cool. He gets a blanket and drapes it around himself to feel more comfortable. He then focuses his intention by remembering his goals for meditation, and especially his goals for improving his health: reducing his neck tension and lowering his blood pressure.

Brian then begins the execution phase. He relaxes briefly by thinking "calm" as he breathes in, and "relaxed" as he breathes out. After a couple of breaths he feels his muscles loosen. Now that he has started to relax, he centers on the phrase, "my arms are heavy and warm." As he does so, he attends to the sensations in his arms. He feels his arms from his shoulders all the way to his fingertips. As he attends to the sensations in his arms, he continues to center on the thought, "my arms are heavy and warm," repeating the phrase in his mind at a comfortable pace.

Brian notices that that his hands feel rather cold, and some discouraging thoughts arise: "I'm not doing it right. This is not working." He remembers, *Let your body do whatever it wants to do. If your arms do not feel heavy or warm, that is OK. The key to this exercise is to "think and let." You think the thought, and let your body do what it wants. If other thoughts come up, just identify them as thoughts and disengage from them. Return to centering on the thought, "my arms are heavy and warm," and accept whatever sensations you are aware of.* Fortunately, Brian has had enough practice with attending to disengage from the discouraging thoughts. He continues to center on the thought, "my arms are heavy and warm." After about another minute, he notices that his right hand feels somewhat warm and comfortable.

Brian continues to think "my arms are heavy and warm" for a couple of minutes, while simply paying attention to the sensations in his arms. Both arms feel a little heavy and his right arm has become comfortably warm. He can also feel a soft, comfortable pulsing in his fingers. It is time to move on to the next step, but he is tempted to continue this one in order to get more heaviness and warmth in his arms. *You must move to the next step after a couple of minutes, even if you do not notice any results. If you extend one step to get more results, you train your body to respond slowly. You also risk trying to get results, and losing the "think and let" attitude. So move on, and the results will come when your body is ready.*

Brian stops centering on the thought, "my arms are heavy and warm," and takes a couple of comfortable breaths. He then begins to think, "my chest is calm and peaceful ... my chest is calm and peaceful . . . my chest is calm and peaceful . . ." As he centers on this thought, he pays attention to the sensations in his chest. He is quite calm and immediately feels a pleasant pulsing in his chest area.

Suddenly, he realizes that he is feeling tense and having worried thoughts about the state of his heart and his high blood pressure. *When you center on the phrase for the chest, you may have anxieties about the state of your heart. Simply identify those thoughts and disengage from them as you go back to centering on the phrase, "my chest is calm and peaceful."*

Brian identifies the anxious thoughts and goes back to centering on the phrase, "my chest is calm and peaceful." He notices the tension decrease and remembers the advice, *Think and let things happen. Your body will take care of you. Center on the phrases gently, attend to the sensations, and trust your body's wisdom.* After a couple of minutes, Brian lets go of the thought "my chest is calm and peaceful," and moves on to the next step.

He takes a couple of deeps breaths and centers on the thought "my breath is free and easy." As he repeats this thought, he pays attention to the sensations in the lower part of his chest, the circular area around the lower edge of his rib cage.

Brian notices that he feels very comfortable and that his breathing is very peaceful. He is enjoying this exercise immensely. After a couple of minutes, he lets go of the thought, "my breath is free and easy," and begins to center on the phrase, "my abdomen is warm and comfortable." As he does so, he attends to the sensations in his abdomen. This is easy for him and, after a couple of minutes, Brian feels the warmth from his abdomen spread all over his body.

Brian moves on to the final step by centering on the thought, "my face is soft and smiling." He feels calm and peaceful all over. His eyes relax and the muscles of his forehead and cheeks smooth out. The corners of his mouth turn up slightly and his jaw loosens. Brian realizes that he usually presents a hard exterior to the world, and this hardness has become a habit, continuing even when he doesn't need it. It feels good to soften his appearance. He enjoys the feeling of a soft smile upon his face, and that deepens the feeling of peace throughout his body.

Brian continues to center on the phrase "my face is soft and smiling," enjoying the sensations in his face. After a couple of minutes, he lets go of that thought and just enjoys the feeling of deep relaxation throughout his body.

Brian moves into the reflection phase of the exercise by reviewing his experience. He remembers that he has to avoid trying to achieve results, and just accept his body's responses as he centers on the different phrases in turn. He notices how warm and comfortable he feels all over, and then gradually reorients himself to time and place. He then takes a deep breath and opens his eyes. *After doing a deep relaxation exercise, remember to get up slowly so that your body has time to adjust to the change in activity.* Brian remembers this advice, and wiggles his fingers and toes before he sits upright, and then stretches his arms and legs before he gets up from the pillow.

Maria's Experience with Autonomic Relaxation

Maria has been looking forward to the health applications. While the basic exercises have helped her somewhat, she wants to get greater benefits. She begins her afternoon session by focusing on her intention: fewer headaches. She then centers on the phrase, "my arms are heavy and warm," while attending to the sensations in her arms. After a few seconds, her mind starts jumping around. She disengages from the distracting thoughts, but they return almost immediately. Maria feels frustrated, but then remembers, *It is OK to have other thoughts during the exercise. Just let the phrase you are centering on be present, as if it were a radio in the background.* Maria finds this helpful, and feels her frustration ease.

After a couple of minutes centering on "my arms are warm and heavy," Maria feels more relaxed. She moves on to the next phrase, "my chest is calm and peaceful," while attending to the sensations in her chest. Again she has to disengage from distracting thoughts, but is able to stay centered.

As Maria centers on the next phrase, "my breath is free and easy," she notices that her breaths are varying in speed and depth. She wonders if he is doing the exercise correctly, because she thinks that she should be breathing deeply if she were relaxed. *Just let your body breathe the way it will. Sometimes, as you relax, your body finds that shorter and shallower breaths are more efficient than slow deep breaths. So the rate and depth of breathing is not directly related to how relaxed you are. Just let the body breathe.* When she remembers this, Maria is able to disengage from the worries about her breath and enjoy the feeling of ease and peace that it gives her. After centering on the thought "my breath is free and easy" for a couple of minutes, she also realizes that her arms are quite comfortable. They have continued to become warmer while she was centering on the other phrases.

When Maria centers on the phrase, "my abdomen is warm and comfortable," she notices that her abdomen actually feels a little bloated and crampy. She tries to continue to center on the phrase, but it feels forced to do so. *If the part of your body associated with the phrase feels uncomfortable, avoid forcing yourself to attend to sensations from that area. Just center on the phrase for a couple of seconds and then move on.*

Maria lets go of trying to pay attention to her abdomen, and moves to the last phrase of the exercise, "my face is soft and smiling." This feels very nice, and seems to reinforce the effect of the previous phrases. Her body feels relaxed from her skin down to deep inside.

Maria reflects on her experience and remembers how many distracting thoughts that she had. She realizes that they did not keep her from doing the exercise and were just a minor annoyance. Maria reorients herself to time and place, and then wiggles her fingers and toes as she ends the exercise.

INSTRUCTIONS FOR AUTONOMIC RELAXATION

This exercise requires proficiency with centering and attending. You will be centering on a mental phrase while attending to sensations. You can start this exercise after you are familiar with the basic exercises from chapters 3 and 4.

1. Start by focusing your intention. Remember your goals for meditation—especially your health goals.
2. Start the execution phase of the exercise by using the brief centering technique from chapter 3; center on the thought "calm" as you inhale and "relaxed" as you exhale. Do this for about five breaths, so that your body settles down a little.
3. Notice your arms, from shoulders to fingertips. Gently attend to the sensations in your arms as you center on the thought, "my arms are heavy and warm." The focus of your awareness is the thought; you should only peripherally be aware of the sensations in your arms. Accept whatever sensations you experience in your arms and continue to center on the thought, "my arms are heavy and warm." If you get distracted by other thoughts or sensations, disengage from these and go back to your center. After two to four minutes, let go of the thought and just enjoy a couple of nice easy breaths.
4. Move your awareness to the sensations in your chest, and center on the thought, "my chest is calm and peaceful." Again, the focus of your awareness is the thought, and you should attend to the sensations in your chest in a peripheral manner. Identify them and let them happen. If other thoughts or sensations come in, simply

notice them, disengage from them, and go back to centering on the thought, "my chest is calm and peaceful." After two to four minutes, let go of the thought, and take a couple of nice easy breaths.

5. Move your awareness to the circular area at the lower edge of your rib cage (the area where your diaphragm is attached). Notice how your lower ribs move outward as you inhale and inward as you exhale. Then center on the thought, "my breath is free and easy." Continue to be gently aware of the sensations at the lower edge of your ribs as you center on this thought. After two to four minutes, let go of the thought and just enjoy a couple of nice easy breaths.
6. Move your awareness to your abdomen. Feel the sensations in your abdomen, from the lower part of the ribs down to the pelvic bones. Also notice how your abdomen is not just in front, but extends to the sides and around to the back. Attend to these sensations as you center on the thought, "my abdomen is warm and comfortable."
7. After two to four minutes of the previous step, allow yourself to enjoy whatever feelings of peace you are experiencing, and center on the phrase, "my face is soft and smiling." Center on this phrase for at least several minutes (you can continue for as long as you like).
8. When you are ready to stop, reflect on your experience. Remember what it was like to center on the different thoughts while watching the sensations and accepting whatever happened. We call this a "think and let" state. In this state you are doing something, without expending effort.

TIPS

Avoid trying to get particular results. If you are anxious about getting results, center more strongly on the mental phrase and pay less attention to the physical sensations.

If a particular phrase causes difficulty, then move on to the next one.

If you have any discomfort from a particular phrase, then do not use it.

If you are being treated for a medical disorder, you must let your physician know that you are doing these exercises, so that any effects can be monitored.

Brian's Results from Autonomic Relaxation

Brian has been practicing autonomic relaxation in four fifteen-minute sessions per week over the preceding month. During the sessions he has noticed that he relaxes more quickly, more deeply, and more consistently. He now feels a much greater sense of ease in his neck and shoulders. At his last visit to the doctor, his blood pressure was still above normal, but it had dropped slightly. His doctor agreed just to watch it for a while before starting any blood-pressure medication. Brian has also learned to use a short version of autonomic relaxation at work. He leans back in his desk chair, and spends twenty to thirty seconds centering on each phrase. This short version takes only two minutes, yet he feels quite relaxed from it. He does this exercise three or fours times per day. These breaks are increasing his mental efficiency and reducing his fatigue.

Maria's Results from Autonomic Relaxation

Maria has practiced autonomic relaxation twice per week for the past two weeks. She does the exercise for about thirty minutes after work. She finds it does relax her, but her mind still gets quite distracted after centering on a phrase for more than about a minute. She described her difficulties to her teacher, who said, *Your mind wants to be active, and that is why it is jumping around. You are experiencing enough relaxation to move on to the next exercise, which will fit your active mind more than this one.* Maria is able to experience a sense of inner relaxation, and the phrase "my face is soft and smiling" feels particularly good to her. She uses it as a brief centering exercise during the day, and finds that it lightens her moods.

INNER HARMONY

Inner harmony builds on autonomic relaxation, and creates a mental state in which we increase the harmony between our minds and our bodies. Most of us have a poor relationship with our bodies. We think of our bodies in very critical terms: we are too fat, too thin, too short, or too tall. Our body does not smell right, move right, or act right. It is not surprising that we are so critical of our bodies, because millions of dollars are spent to convince us that something is wrong with them. After all, if we were happy with our bodies, then we wouldn't spend billions of dollars to try to change them.

Spend a little time attending to the thoughts that go through your head about your body. Are they warm, friendly, complimentary thoughts? Or are they harsh, critical, and even abusive thoughts? What if you lived with someone who was as critical of you as you are of your body? How would you react if others complimented or thanked you as rarely as you compliment or thank your body?

The exercise of inner harmony changes this. In this exercise, you will apply your concentrating and attending skills toward developing a warm, accepting, and loving relationship with your body. When your body feels loved, then it works more harmoniously with you. All the systems within the body will work more harmoniously as well.

In the inner harmony technique, you start with the experience of relaxation that you obtained from autonomic relaxation. Then, you concentrate on a sense of love and gratitude. As you concentrate on that sense of love and gratitude, you think about the processes your body carries out, and about how all the different parts of your body participate in these processes to keep you alive and healthy.

These processes are respiration, digestion, purification, sensation, expression, and regulation. You need not learn all the details about how the processes work. Your mind knows the details in a more profound way, and you can trust it. You simply need to think about each process in turn, while concentrating on the feeling of love and gratitude for each.

By concentrating on love and gratitude while thinking about the different processes in the body, you help your body's systems feel loved and facilitate their working together.

Brian's Experience with Inner Harmony

Brian is beginning an inner harmony session after a month of practicing autonomic relaxation, which he greatly enjoyed. He focuses his intention to feel more healthy, and then begins the execution stage by taking two minutes to go rapidly through autonomic relaxation. As he centers on the phrase "my face is soft and smiling," he feels very quiet and peaceful inside. Brian then thinks about feeling love and gratitude for his body. Nothing much seems to come to him. He just feels quiet inside, without much emotion. *If your mind is so quiet that it doesn't feel love and gratitude, then you have to wake it up a bit. Think about having a body and what would happen if you didn't have one. This can generate more energy.* Brian realizes that he is glad that his body works as well as it does. He doesn't usually think about it and tends to take it for granted. He scans his body mentally and feels warm and happy about it.

As Brian thinks about the process of respiration, he feels somewhat uncomfortable. His mind doesn't want to think about all the details. It just wants to stay with the warm and happy feeling. *When doing this exercise, you are bringing a feeling of love to the processes of your body. You don't need to think about the individual parts. The essence of the process of respiration is the generation of energy. Just think about your body generating energy.* Brian finds it easier to think about energy, rather than various body parts he doesn't know much about. He thinks about how all the cells in his body use energy, and feels thankful that they are able to do that. After a couple of minutes, he feels a little tingly all over.

Brian moves on to the next process, digestion. He remembers to focus on the process and not the parts. He thinks about his cells getting nutrients and experiences a sense of fullness. He then focuses on the process of purification, thinking about how his body cleanses itself of things that are harmful. He feels love and gratitude toward his body for doing that. After a few minutes, he feels as if a fluid is washing through him.

When Brian moves to the next process, sensation, he begins to feel a little tired. He is finding the inner harmony exercise difficult, and prefers autonomic relaxation. He wants to stop thinking about all these processes and just rest in a state of quiet and relaxation. *If your mind has a lot of natural steadiness, you will enjoy autonomic relaxation more. You do need to practice inner harmony so that you can improve your relationship with your body. Experiencing the sense of love and gratitude for your body is very important. If you are feeling tired, move though the systems more quickly.* Brian thinks briefly about the different sensory processes and how grateful he is that he can see, hear, touch, taste, and smell. After a couple of minutes, he focuses on the process of expression, and then moves to the process of regulation. He finds that the exercise feels more effective if he thinks about each process briefly and then recenters on the feeling of peace, gratitude, and love associated with the smile on his face.

Maria's Experience with Inner Harmony

Maria has been encouraged by the positive change in her health that she has obtained so far. She has practiced autonomic relaxation for a couple of weeks. She is able to move through the different phrases rapidly, and during the day has used "my face is soft and smiling" as a brief technique. She is looking forward to the next exercise, inner harmony.

Maria starts by focusing her intention. She remembers her goals for meditation and focuses specifically on her goal of improving her health, and having fewer headaches.

Maria starts the execution phase by going rapidly through autonomic relaxation. She spends a few seconds centering on each of the first five phrases. She has been practicing this exercise for a couple of weeks, and so she is able to relax quickly. She then centers on the phrase "my face is soft and smiling" for a couple of minutes, to deepen the sense of peace and relaxation.

Once you have completed the autonomic relaxation exercise, center on the phrase, "my face is soft and smiling." Let yourself feel a sense of peace all over your body. Think about how thankful you are that you have a body. It can help to remember a time when you felt thankful, peaceful, and happy. Maria remembers an afternoon in the park with her family. The sun was shining, the air was warm, and the temperature was just right. Her children were playing peacefully together on the grass, and she and her husband had an enjoyable time. As Maria remembers the scene, she smiles and feels a sense of relaxation around her eyes, almost as if her eyes are smiling.

Having connected with the emotions of peace and gratitude, Maria thinks about how much work her body does for her and how thankful she is for that. She feels love and gratitude for her body, and her smile deepens as she feels even more peaceful.

Maria then begins to think about the different body processes in turn. She first reflects on the process of respiration. This is the process by which her body takes in oxygen and uses it to produce energy. She thinks about how her lungs and diaphragm work together to breathe in the oxygen. She thinks about how her blood cells pick up the oxygen, and how her heart pumps the blood to all the parts of the body.

Maria starts to feel that she is losing the sense of peace and gratitude as she gets more involved in thinking about the process of respiration. *Continue to reinforce the sense of love and gratitude by returning your awareness to the feeling of smiling in your face and eyes. Let those sensations anchor you to the more abstract idea of love and thankfulness for your body.*

Maria returns her awareness to her smile and the emotions of love and gratitude. She then goes back to reflecting on the process of respiration, realizing that the oxygen delivered to the cells is used by them to produce energy, energy that helps them live and carry out their functions. She suddenly has the sense that all her cells are humming happily as they use the oxygen brought to them by the blood, and that her lungs, heart, and blood vessels are humming as well, in tune with her cells.

Maria then lets go of thinking about the process of respiration, and returns to her feeling of gratitude by focusing her attention on the sensation of smiling in her face. After a couple of comfortable breaths, she moves on to the next process, digestion.

Maria thinks about the process by which her body extracts nutrients from food and sends it to all the cells in her body. As she starts thinking about all the organs involved in digestion, she starts to worry that she doesn't know enough about them. *You need not know all the parts of the body that are involved. Think about the process, the idea of digestion, and not all the biochemical steps.*

Maria lets go of struggling to remember all the digestive organs, and thinks about the activity they all contribute to: extracting nutrients out of food, converting them into forms her cells can use, and transporting them all over her body. She develops a feeling of satisfaction, as if her cells are comfortable and satiated.

Maria lets go of thinking about digestion and moves on to the next process, purification. This is the process by which her body gets rid of everything that is useless or harmful, and by which it replaces worn-out parts. The first thing that leaps to mind is her intestines and kidneys, which excrete solid and liquid waste. This seems to be a distasteful idea, but she quickly realizes that she is thankful for those organs, as she would be very uncomfortable if they did not do their work correctly. *If you feel some aversion toward a particular process or part of your body, then you need to work on bringing love and gratitude there. Reinforce your connection to the love and gratitude by being aware of the smile on your face.*

Maria reinforces her sense of gratitude by focusing her attention on the gentle smile in her face, and then continues to think about the process of purification. She realizes that her immune cells are part of this process because they get rid of harmful invaders. They also break down old, worn-out cells, making room for the body to replace them. As she brings the sense of peace into the process of purification, Maria feels a sense of cleansing, as if some fluid or energy is washing through her. She realizes that even her skin gets rid of salts, and so it too is involved in this purification process. She enjoys the feeling of cleansing and feels even more peaceful.

Maria then thinks about the process of sensation. She thinks briefly about each of the senses. She feels grateful for her ability to see, hear, smell, taste, and touch. She reflects on how each of these senses brings joy to her life. She feels gratitude for her ability to sense the beauty around her. As she experiences this, she feels more connected to her world.

Maria thinks about the process of expression. She reflects on the different ways she expresses herself and how her body helps her to do that. At first she is confused about the parts of the body that contribute to that process. *You use your muscles, bones, and the connections between them to gesture, speak, draw, write, and perform all other activities by which you communicate.* As Maria reflects on this, she realizes that even her breathing muscles are involved in the process of expression because they bring in the air that she uses to speak with. She remembers hearing that her vocal cords are muscles as well, and that their relaxation and contraction changes the pitch of her voice. She thinks about her smile, and realizes that it comes from the way that the muscles of her face move. As Maria does this, she feels a new appreciation for her body and her muscles. She had thought of muscles as important only for lifting weight, and more of a male thing. Now, however, she sees them as the means by which she expresses herself. The thought of muscles being feminine is new to her. Maria feels a sense of warmth flow through her and feels a friendliness with her body that she hasn't felt before.

Maria moves to the last process in the exercise, that of regulation. She reflects on all the different processes that are going on at once inside her, and on how she is also aware of and communicating with the world outside of her body. She thinks about how all these processes are regulated so that they work harmoniously. She realizes that communication among all the different cells in her body is a vital part of this process. *It is very likely that every cell in our body receives some form of information from every other cell. The different parts of the body are not isolated. Our body processes have a natural flow and rhythm that is wonderful.* Maria reflects on how often she feels as if she is isolated from her body, and on how she dislikes certain parts of her body. She realizes that all the parts of her body are intimately connected with each other. She thinks about how they must communicate with each other to regulate their activity into a harmonious flow. As Maria does this, she feels warm and accepting of her whole physical being. She has an image of how interconnected it is, and of how many different processes flow in cycles. She thinks about the different cycles she goes through, daily cycles and monthly cycles, and reflects on the extraordinary communication that regulates those. Maria feels as if her body is humming like a networked telephone system, with everything inside communicating with everything else.

Maria rests in this peaceful state for some time before her alarm beeps at her. She then reflects on the wonderful sense of gratitude she feels for her body. She thinks about how she takes her body for granted most of the time, noticing it only to scold it for something. In contrast, this experience feels quite pleasant, and she plans to practice the inner harmony technique frequently.

INSTRUCTIONS FOR INNER HARMONY

1. Start out with the autonomic relaxation exercise. You should be able to move through all the phrases, getting some relaxation from each, within two to five minutes.
2. While you center on "my face is soft and smiling," think about love and gratitude. It may help you in connecting with this sense of love and gratitude to remember a time when you felt these emotions. You will know you are successful when you feel a soft smile appear effortlessly on your face.
3. Once you feel love and gratitude, think about how grateful you are for having a body. Thank your body for being there, and staying alive for you.
4. Concentrate on the emotions of love and gratitude while you think about each of your body's processes in turn. If you get distracted from the sense of love and gratitude, refresh your memory by returning your awareness to the smile on your face.
5. As you think about the processes, do not worry if you are unsure of all the different parts involved. Just as you can enjoy music without knowing exactly how all the instruments work, you can feel gratitude for your

body processes without knowing all the anatomy and physiology involved.

6. Concentrate on each of the following processes for two to four minutes in turn.

Respiration—This is the process by which your body produces energy. Your lungs, heart, and blood are involved, of course, but all your body cells are also involved because they use oxygen, sugar, and fat to generate energy. Imagine that each cell in your body is a little power plant and that all these cells are generating energy.

Digestion—This is the process by which your body extracts nutrients from your food and delivers them to the cells. The body parts involved are the mouth, teeth, stomach, and intestines. The liver and pancreas also participate by making chemicals that help digest the food. The heart and blood help by transporting the nutrients all over the body. Think about how all the cells in your body are receiving the nutrients that they need.

Purification—This is the process by which your body gets rid of everything that is useless or harmful to it. It also includes the processes by which your body replaces worn-out parts. The most obvious organs involved are the kidneys and intestines. However, the lungs are involved because they breathe out carbon dioxide. The immune system has an important role in purification because it is constantly cleansing the body of harmful organisms. Think about the process of cleansing that is constantly going on throughout your body.

Sensation—This includes the processes by which you receive information from the world around you. Sensation requires the five sense organs: eyes, ears, nose, tongue, and skin. It also includes the nerves that give us position sense, and our sense of movement. Think about the process of perceiving beauty around you.

Expression—This is the process by which we communicate with and influence the world. The parts of the body involved include the muscles, ligaments, tendons and bones. Also remember the facial muscles and muscles of the vocal cords. The brain is involved as the coordinating center. Think about the process of connecting with the world around you.

Regulation—This is the process by which your body coordinates all its other activities. It involves the whole nervous system, including the parts of the nervous system that regulate autonomic functions such as blood pressure, gastric movements, heart rate, and resting muscle tone. It also includes the glands that secrete hormones: pituitary, hypothalamus, thyroid, adrenals, and sex organs. Think about all the cells in your body communicating with each other.

Brian's Results from Inner Harmony

Brian has worked with inner harmony over the last two weeks, but he still feels it is too much work to think about each of the processes in detail. He has taken his teacher's advice, and just thinks briefly about each process and then returns to concentrating on the sense of love and gratitude for his body. This is increasing his sense of peace with himself and is lowering his chronic stress level.

Maria's Results from Inner Harmony

After one month of practicing inner harmony twice per week, Maria realizes that her breathing has naturally become smoother. As her breathing has become smoother, she has found her physical movements becoming more coordinated as well. Maria is now able to catch her headaches coming on, before her head actually starts to hurt. This helps her to stop them effectively, either by doing a brief relaxation exercise, or by taking her medicine sooner.

Maria also has discovered that if she focuses on peace and gratitude and thinks about the process of digestion after eating, then she feels more satisfied and her abdomen feels more comfortable.

HEALING LIGHT

Many traditions speak of the healing properties of light. Healers often speak about seeing certain patterns of light when they work with people. Modern physics indicates that matter can be thought of as condensed light; so, light is a powerful healing image that is also connected to your physical form.

When you do this exercise, you will be using your attending, concentrating, and opening skills to evoke the experience of a healing light. You will then bring the image into your body, so that you can experience the idea of good health on a deep physical level.

Focusing your intention at the beginning of the exercise is very important. Your intention tells your mind what to create. If you do not focus your intention, your mind can create an image that has nothing to do with improving your health. It is your intention that gives coherence to the experiences your mind will produce.

After focusing your intention, concentrate on the idea of good health. Concentrating on the idea of good health enables you to experience what is otherwise an abstract idea. As you concentrate on the idea of good health, identify and disengage from any particular images that arise. Eventually the images will begin to dissolve into an experience of light or colors. The light is what you will work with, because it will contain all of the images and bring their positive energy into your body.

Brian's Experience with Healing Light

Brian has practiced inner harmony enough times that he can feel love and gratitude for his body. He is ready to move on to the next technique. Brian starts by lying down and covering himself with a blanket. *The healing light application can create a very altered state of consciousness. It helps to practice lying down, so that you can completely let go.* He then focuses his intention by remembering his goals for meditation and his goal for this session: experiencing a deep sense of health and healing.

Brian has been practicing so often that as soon as he does these things, his body is already settling down. After a couple of easy breaths, he is quite relaxed. He centers on the thought "my face is soft and smiling" for a couple of minutes, and then concentrates on the feeling of love and gratitude for his body. As he feels his body respond to that love and gratitude, Brian moves into the practice of healing light.

Brian concentrates on the idea of excellent health. As he does so, he realizes that the idea seems rather abstract—he doesn't have a clear sense of what it means. As his mind starts to feel confused, he remembers his teacher saying, *Getting a clear sense of excellent health can be difficult. It can help to think about the results of excellent health. Think about how your body would feel if you were exceptionally healthy—how easy it would be to breathe, how your heart would be strong, how your whole body would be vibrant, and all the cells in it would be alive.* Brian remembers various events from his life—playing basketball with friends, swimming in the ocean, hiking in the mountains. His mind moves from one event to another, and he remembers feeling strong and flexible, being able to breath deeply and easily with his heart pumping strongly. Brian suddenly realizes that he is feeling somewhat regretful; he misses the way that he used to feel. *Remember that you are using the memory simply to evoke the idea of excellent health. If other thoughts or emotions come up, simply identify them, disengage from them, and return your concentration to the sense of feeling healthy. If this is too difficult, then return to practicing the exercise you started with, autonomic relaxation or inner harmony.*

Brian identifies his feelings as regrets, and goes back to concentrating on the body sensations of feeling healthy. He remembers his experiences with autonomic relaxation and how good that exercise felt. Brian relaxes more and more, and his thoughts are positive. He is thinking about how good he feels and how he enjoys being healthy.

As he concentrates on the internal sensations of feeling healthy, images come to mind. He sees an eagle flying through the air, then the face of a wolf appears. He sees runners competing in a race, and hears the sound of the ocean. *As you focus your mind on the idea of excellent health, it will often produce images. They are symbolic representations of your experiences of health. In this exercise, you will move to a level beneath the symbols, so avoid analyzing these images. Just notice them in an accepting manner, then let them go and return to the feeling of health.*

Brian disengages from the images and returns to concentrating on the idea of health. As he does so, the images gradually fade. Soon everything seems to be getting dark. Brian waits for a bit, but nothing appears. He wonders if he has done something wrong. *After the images fade, there is often a period of darkness. Remember that your intention at the beginning of the session was to experience a healing light, and wait for what appears. Sometimes people experience the healing light as darkness. As long as you stay connected with the idea of health and feel peaceful, you are doing fine.*

Brian continues to concentrate on the feeling of health, and remembers his intention at the beginning of the session to experience a healing light. At first, more images appear, but they pass as he disengages from them. Soon he is experiencing just a variety of colors in various shapes. He continues to concentrate on the idea of health while he watches the colors in his mind's eye.

Brian suddenly finds himself aware of a bright yellow light that fills his whole inner vision. He remembers someone saying that white light is for healing. Then he remembers someone else saying that green represents health. He begins to worry that he is seeing the wrong color. *Accept the color that your mind gives you. There are no absolute rules about which colors to use; each individual's experience is different. You may see any color or combination of colors. The colors may change when you repeat the exercise. Just concentrate on the idea of health, and allow your mind to create the color it wants to use for the occasion.*

Brian is reassured, and pays attention to the yellow light. It feels warm and comforting, and seems to resonate with the feeling of health that he was experiencing. He lets go of concentrating on the feeling of health and opens to the yellow light. He remembers the feeling of vastness he experienced during the opening exercises, and feels space inside himself. As he does this, he imagines the yellow light flowing into that space completely.

Brian imagines the light filling his head, neck, shoulders, arms, chest, abdomen, pelvis, and legs. He allows himself to feel more and more inner space, and imagines the yellow light filling it. Soon, he is feeling the yellow light as a warm, physical, healing substance inside himself.

As he continues to concentrate on the yellow light while feeling the space inside himself, he loses track of his body size and shape. He feels like he has become a ball of yellow light that is swirling and moving in beautiful patterns. He just enjoys the experience, every now and then remembering his intention of experiencing good health.

After his watch alarm beeps to signal the end of the session, Brian reflects on how peaceful the experience was. He appreciates how his mind was able to create the image of light, once he trusted it. He reorients to time and place by remembering his physical surroundings, and then reorients to his body by wiggling his fingers and toes, and flexing and stretching his arms and legs for a few seconds before opening his eyes.

Maria's Experience with Healing Light

Maria is starting her first session with the healing light technique. She focuses her intention and then goes rapidly through the inner harmony technique. This takes her about five minutes, and she feels peaceful and relaxed. Maria then concentrates on the idea of excellent health. She experiences a feeling of vibrancy and energy in her body. She imagines being bouncy and vivacious, enjoying life and having plenty of energy to accomplish the day's tasks.

As Maria does this, she feels more and more comfortable. She remembers her intention for the session was to experience a healing light. A series of images appears and disappears. She stays disengaged from thoughts and images, and feels as if she is floating peacefully. Maria focuses on her intention to experience a healing light again, and then remembers the sense of expansion and contraction she felt during her opening practice sessions. Soon she feels the familiar space and vastness inside her body. She remembers her intention to experience a healing light. Suddenly she is aware of a blue light inside her. As she notices it, it changes to yellow, then green, then red, and then back to blue. Then a yellow stripe appears, followed by some green swirls. Maria remembers, *The color of the light does not really matter. It is OK if the color changes, or if there are several colors at once. Remember your intention every now and then, and continue to experience the vastness and space and let the colors do what they will.*

Maria disengages from trying to stabilize the colors, and just enjoys the experience. The colors continue to flow and change, and this seems to enhance the experience of openness. She feels as if her whole body is a huge, rainbow-colored ball. After enjoying this for awhile, Maria realizes that her alarm is beeping. It is time to finish. She reflects on how focusing her intention and then letting go was effective in giving her a very enjoyable experience. She then reorients to time and place, wiggles her fingers and toes, flexes her arms and legs and takes a deep breath before she opens her eyes.

INSTRUCTIONS FOR HEALING LIGHT

This application uses attending, concentrating, and opening skills. The exercise takes between twenty and forty minutes to complete.

You will not be completely in control of how long it will take, so you should set aside at least forty minutes to do the exercise.

1. Start by sitting or lying in a comfortable position in which you can relax completely. Be sure to be warm.
2. Focus your intention to experience a feeling of health as deeply as possible.
3. Concentrate on the idea of excellent health. One way of doing this is to remember a time when you felt great, when your whole body was in excellent shape. Another way is to think about what excellent health would feel like. Use your concentrating skills to increase the strength of this feeling. The goal of this step is to experience the idea of excellent health as clearly as possible.
4. If specific memories or images come, identify and disengage from them. Continue to concentrate on the idea of excellent health.
5. When you feel a connection with the idea of excellent health, pay attention to any colors that are appearing. If you are having images or memories, pay attention to the colors in the images. If your visual field is dark, just wait expectantly. Ask your mind to create a color that represents the idea of excellent health that you are feeling. Continue to concentrate on the feeling of health, while just watching the colors that appear. Trust your mind to create the color(s) that are right for you. Remember that black is a color, too, and it may be the right one for you.
6. Open to that healing light. Remember the sense of vastness from the opening exercises, and allow the healing light to fill it. Let go of concentrating on the idea of

excellent health, and concentrate on the image of light while experiencing the vastness.

7. Imagine the light filling your whole body. Your body may feel like it has changed size or shape. That does not matter, just allow the light to fill everywhere that feels like part of you. Imagine the light filling this space fully.
8. Continue to experience the light flowing and moving through the space. Every now and then, remember your intention to have excellent health.
9. You may lose track of your usual body dimensions, and you may lose track of time. When you finish the session, reflect on your experience, and then reorient yourself gradually to the time and place, and to your body.

Brian's Results from Healing Light

Brian practices the healing light exercise once per week for a month. He also practices autonomic relaxation once per week. He rotates through the basic exercises of attending, concentrating, and opening during his other sessions.

At the end of the month, his wife points out to him that he has made some positive changes in his diet. He is eating smaller portions, and is skipping dessert frequently. When he hears that, Brian realizes that he has not been eating the donuts during the Friday morning meetings at work, either. He is amazed that he has made these changes without trying or even noticing. It is as though his mind is automatically acting in accord with the intention for better health that he focuses on at the beginning of the healing light technique. When he goes for his scheduled visit to the doctor a couple of days later, he is pleasantly surprised to find that he has lost three pounds and that his blood pressure has decreased slightly.

Maria's Results from Healing Light

Over a period of three weeks, Maria practices inner harmony and healing light once per week each, and practices the basic attending, concentrating, and opening techniques once each. At the end of that time, she notices that she is taking life a lot more easily. She is not as insistent about keeping things in order. This more easygoing attitude has coincided with an almost complete elimination of her headaches. She asks her teacher about this. *It is common for illnesses to be made worse by things that are not directly related to the disease process: lifestyle, emotions, behaviors, or attitudes. It is hard to discover these indirect causes by thinking about the disease directly. Or, you come up with too many indirect causes. By using the mental quality of spaciousness, the healing light experience allows your mind to find and change those things that are indirectly related to the illness. This naturally leads to improvement.*

CONCLUSION

As you practice these applications, your body will become more resistant to the pressures of the fast-paced modern world. You will feel more peaceful and coherent; healthier, more energetic, and more comfortable.

The three health applications we have described should be used in sequence. They require different abilities and have different effects. Autonomic relaxation uses centering and attending skills to create a deep state of relaxation that allows your body to heal faster and recover from fatigue. Inner harmony uses attending and concentrating skills to create a positive relationship between you and your body. It counters the common messages received from advertising that your body is defective. You can experience your body as wonderful, even if it is not "perfect." Healing light uses attending, concentrating, and opening skills to evoke an altered state of consciousness that can create healing in indirect ways.

You should become familiar enough with autonomic relaxation to be able to do it easily and quickly before moving to inner harmony (once you can do autonomic relaxation and get relaxed within five minutes, you are ready to move on). You can then continue to practice autonomic relaxation as a brief technique.

As you acquire more skill with inner harmony, you will be able to move through that application more quickly as well. Then you can use it, too, as a brief technique, several times a day, thereby maintaining a positive attitude toward your body.

Once you can consistently experience the positive attitude toward your body during the inner harmony exercise, you are ready to move to healing light. Practice the healing light exercise one or two times per week. You can practice autonomic relaxation or inner harmony in one or two extended sessions per week, as well.

It usually takes one or two months to experience success with these three applications. When you move on to one of the other sets of applications, you can maintain your health gains by continuing to practice brief versions of autonomic relaxation or inner harmony a couple of times during each day.

nine

performance: moving into "the zone"

If the bow's string is too tight, loosen it; tighten or loosen it as needed, making sure that it does not get too loose. In the end, the sound of music will be sweet.

The Buddha

Enhanced performance entails more than just doing better at something. In order to enhance your performance in a profound sense, you must do better without burning out. You must use your energy without getting used up. And, equally, you must know how to focus on those activities that are truly fulfilling.

When you use meditation to enhance your performance, you take a big step toward finding peace amid the pressures of modern life. You learn to increase your abilities by staying calm when pressure builds, and to use visualization so that your unconscious mind can work on several tasks at once. You are able to get past blocks, so that you can stop spinning your wheels and move forward.

Meditation literature is full of stories about people who have used meditation to enhance their performance. Many athletes use meditation to improve their skills, and many of our students have used it to help them do better both on the playing field and at work. You, too, can use meditation to increase your performance at physical and mental tasks.

Physical performance is just one aspect of performance that is enhanced with meditation; mental performance can be increased as well. The basic exercises that you have been practicing develop memory, concentration, flexible thinking, abstract reasoning, and creativity. These mental skills will be augmented by meditation applications. In today's world, work performance is associated more with mental skills than physical ability. By increasing your mental performance, you will improve your effectiveness and efficiency at work.

There are several ways to enhance performance using meditation. You will learn three applications, each of which will enhance your performance in a different manner. The first application, heightened focus, enables you to maintain an alert and calm state, even when under pressure. If you are too anxious while doing a task, your performance will suffer and you will use more energy than necessary. If you are too relaxed while doing a task, you will not be energized enough to do well. Meditation helps you be energized for a task while staying calm and unstressed. This is taught in the heightened focus application.

Meditation also helps you by improving your imagination. Your imagination is so powerful that if you vividly imagine doing something well, your mind can learn from the experience as though you had actually performed the task. This is called mental rehearsal, or visualization. Meditation improves your ability to visualize, and increases the power of the visualizations. After you have learned directed imagination, you will be able to practice visualizing without having to concentrate on the process. You will be able to visualize a successful result even while performing other tasks.

Finally, many people have internal blocks that keep them from succeeding. These obstacles can come from negative programming, fears about what success will lead to, or pursuing inappropriate goals. By using the clearing blocks application, you will be able to move around obstacles, or to recognize when their existence is due to pursuit of the wrong goals.

HEIGHTENED FOCUS

Imagine being totally focused on a task and feeling so calm that your performance is effortless. That is what heightened focus will enable you to experience. To do well under pressure, you must be highly alert and calm at the same time.

Staying calm and alert simultaneously is difficult, especially under pressure. Many people become more nervous as they get more alert, and they get less alert when they become calm. By learning to become extremely alert and focused while staying calm, you can bring more energy to your tasks in a coherent manner.

This technique uses your centering and attending skills to help you stay focused on your task while disengaging from distractions. When you are absorbed in a task, you are not aware of distractions and your energy is completely devoted to performing the task. Some people describe this state as "being in the zone."

When you are in that focused, calm state, you can accomplish far more with less energy. Your body and mind work much more efficiently. This helps you to remain peaceful because you are meeting your responsibilities more easily. In fact, the experience can even generate energy, so that you complete a task feeling more energized than when you started.

Heightened focus is something that you do while engaged in a task. It should not be done in extended sessions away from the event you want to work on. To do the technique, you will center your awareness on something that is centrally related to your task. You will maintain a continuous awareness of that aspect of the task while staying peripherally aware of your surroundings. You will then identify and disengage from any thoughts, sensations, or emotions that hinder you in completing the task. This uses centering and attending skills to focus your awareness to a higher state.

Finding something appropriate to center on can be tricky. You must find something that is related to your task and that will not distract you. Here are a few examples to clarify this concept. If you were playing tennis, you might center on the ball; if you were running, you might center on the image of the finish, or on a feeling of strength in your legs. If you were writing, you might center on the points that you wanted to make, or on the idea that you wanted to convey.

Once you have chosen something to center on, you should maintain a continuous awareness of it. If anything distracts you, identify it. The distractions are often thoughts, but they can be sensations or emotions as well. If the distraction is helpful, adjust to it; if it is not helpful, disengage from it and go back to your original center. For example, if you were playing tennis and noticed that your opponent had moved out of position on the court, this would be a helpful observation. On the other hand, thoughts about not doing well would be unhelpful, and you should disengage from them and return to centering your awareness on the ball. As you practice, your mind will automatically avoid unhelpful distractions and increase its awareness of things that are helpful.

Brian's Experience with Heightened Focus

Brian's performance goal was to improve his golf game. He has noticed some improvement from practicing the basic exercises, but he wants to do better. He knows that he tends to tense up when he is making a shot, and he hopes that practicing heightened focus can reduce this.

The next time he tees off, he centers on the golf ball. As he looks at it he keeps his mind alert, and he becomes aware of a number of thoughts that were previously hidden. "Wonder if you'll drive it short. Don't slice it off to the left. Watch out for the water trap." His mind acts like an overly concerned parent giving him unneeded advice. Brian identifies these thoughts as unhelpful distractions. Because of his experience with attending meditation, he is able to disengage from them and center again on the ball.

As he maintains his focus on the ball, he notices an increasing number of body sensations. He can feel how his weight is balanced on his feet, and sense the position of his hips and shoulders in relation to the club more clearly than before. He identifies these sensations as helpful, and by noticing them while maintaining awareness of the ball, he feels his alertness increase. He becomes gradually more aware of his body, the ball, and the relationship between them. Brian then becomes aware of how his golf partner is looking at him. He identifies this as an unhelpful distraction, and disengages from it, refocusing on the ball.

As Brian disengages from distractions, he feels that he has more energy focused on hitting the ball. His energy feels coherent and not as scattered. The club seems to swing forward on its own without much effort, and the ball takes off from the tee.

Brian continues to use this technique as he plays the next eight holes. Sometimes he feels that he is straining to maintain his focus on the ball. He remembers, *Maintain a gentle focus on the ball. You are to center on the ball, which means that your focus is gentle, not too intense. You get a gentle focus not by concentrating harder on the ball, but by disengaging from distractions. This way the only things that you are paying attention to are sensations, thoughts, and emotions that are related to your task.* Brian has a few instances when he feels this happen. It is an experience of being totally focused, not just on the ball, but on everything related to hitting it. The rest of the world seems to disappear.

Brian notices that when he has this calm and alert focus, the ball goes farther and straighter than usual. He starts straining to make that happen, and his shots get worse. *Do not strain to make this happen. The key is to disengage from distractions. The desire to make the technique work is a powerful distraction, so disengage from that, too. Accept the fact that it takes practice to become more consistent.* Brian remembers to be patient with himself and not to try to make a huge improvement overnight.

Maria's Experience with Heightened Focus

Maria's performance goal is to improve her presentations at work. Though she has become calmer throughout much of the workday because of practicing the basic exercises, she still gets nervous when giving presentations. She either forgets some of the points that she wants to make, or she focuses on them and presents in a rapid, flustered style that loses most of her audience. Maria wasn't sure how to practice the technique before she actually gave the presentation. Her teacher advised, *You could give trial presentations and practice the technique then, but it would be better to use the technique in a situation that occurs more frequently. Are there any other situations in which you feel the same way, tense and flustered about saying something in front of others?*

Maria realizes that she feels this way when she makes comments or asks questions in a meeting. She decides that she can practice the heightened focus technique when in meetings, so that she will be familiar with it and able to use it when she makes presentations.

In the next meeting, Maria wants to ask a question and feels the familiar tension come up. She centers on the question, keeping her awareness on it. At the same time, she attends to what is distracting her and disengages from it. At first she feels tightness in her stomach and weakness in her legs. As she disengages from these and goes back to centering on the question, she notices a number of thoughts that she had been unaware of. Part of her mind is thinking, "That's a stupid question. People will think you are really dumb."

These thoughts are difficult to disengage from, so Maria identifies the activity her mind is doing as "criticizing." Identifying the process helps her to disengage from the thoughts and return to centering on the question she wants to ask.

This process has taken a few seconds, and now that the distractions are fewer, Maria is more aware of other people and the comments that they are making. She feels more present in the room, and understands how her question involves something that other people also are having difficulty understanding. As she speaks, she notices that her tone of voice is firmer and her body feels stronger than it usually does. The speaker responds politely to her question, and Maria feels pleased by the experience.

INSTRUCTIONS FOR HEIGHTENED FOCUS

This application should be done during the relevant event or performance.

1. Focus on your intention. Get a clear idea of what you want to improve, and set that as your goal.
2. Center on something central to succeeding at your immediate task. Finding the appropriate thing to center on can be difficult. Trial and error may be necessary. Some examples may help:

   In sports such as golf or tennis, center on the ball; in endurance sports such as swimming or running, center on the image of the finish, or on the image of being full of energy; for taking a test, center on each question in turn; while giving a talk or writing, center on the major points that you want to make.

   Maintain continuous awareness of your center.
3. Attend to thoughts, sensations, and emotions that arise. If they are helpful, incorporate them into your awareness. If they are unhelpful, disengage from them and bring your awareness back to your center. Continue this as long as you are not straining.
4. After the event, reflect on your experience, and note any patterns in the distracting thoughts or sensations.

Brian and Maria's Results with Heightened Focus

After a couple of weeks, Brian is able to achieve heightened focus consistently. He feels more energized and relaxed after a round of golf, and has lowered his score by a couple of strokes. He is not sure if this will continue, and sometimes he wonders if it is just luck. But he is enjoying the game more, and is less critical of himself.

After using the heightened focus technique during several meetings, Maria notices that she is naturally feeling.more confident when speaking in front of others. She has a presentation coming up in three weeks, and hopes that this and the next meditation application will make a big difference.

DIRECTED IMAGINATION

Your imagination is so powerful that if you imagine something vividly enough, then you will experience it as a real event. For example, if you imagine washing your hands in warm water, your hands will warm up. This ability of your imagination allows you to use it to improve your performance. If you vividly imagine successful performances, your mind will learn from them just as if they had occurred. As far as your mind is concerned, the events did occur.

This technique is often called visualization. We dislike that term because it restricts imagination to visual experiences. Many people imagine sounds, movements, or feelings better then visual images. You need not have a visual experience in order to use this technique.

Directed imagination uses attending and concentrating skills; the concentrating skills are especially important. Because you have practiced the basic concentrating exercise, you will be able to direct your imagination in the correct manner without straining it. The brief concentrating exercise that you have been practicing—in which you remember an event from earlier in the day—is also helpful. It teaches you to imagine in all sensory modalities, and to do so quickly.

Directed imagination has an extended and a brief version. During the extended sessions, you will vividly imagine a successful performance. In the brief sessions, you will condense that successful imagination into a few seconds, and recall it frequently throughout the day, enabling your mind to keep training while you do other tasks.

The most important point in using directed imagination successfully is that you must imagine success. If you imagine a different result, then you will not train your mind to be successful. This may seem obvious, but we have worked with people who were not precise about what they imagined. Their images had elements of failure in them, and the technique did not work as well. This is why you need concentrating and attending skills to use the technique. Concentrating allows you to vividly imagine the experience, and attending allows you to identify and disengage from any elements of the image that are not consistent with the successful result you want to imagine.

Brian's Experience with Directed Imagination

Brian knows that he could improve his golf game significantly by learning to putt more consistently and accurately. He wants to use directed imagination to improve his putting. His teacher advises, *Imagine putting the golf ball successfully. You may see yourself doing that in your mind's eye, but you should use your other senses as well. Imagine the sounds, the smells, the feel of the club in your hands, and the position and movement of your body. You can connect to the image of putting well by remembering a couple of successful putts. This is similar to the brief concentrating technique.*

Brian begins the extended session by sitting comfortably and focusing his intention to putt more accurately. He relaxes, and remembers standing on the green, holding the putter, and looking at the ball. The image of the green takes a few minutes to develop, almost as if it were a photograph. Brian experiences bits and pieces of the experience. He sees the ball and the green, he feels the warm sun on his back. He smells the clean air and feels the touch of the light breeze. He feels the roughness of the putter's handle on his palms and feels the weight of it in his hands. He imagines swinging the club, and sees the ball roll smoothly and come to rest just to the left of the cup. He identifies this as an unsuccessful result, and disengages from it by imagining the experience before he hit the ball. He then imagines hitting the ball again, and again it misses the cup. Brian is frustrated. How is he going to use this technique when he can't imagine success? *If you try to imagine success and you experience failure in the image, you may be trying to imagine something that is too difficult for you at this time. Imagine success at something easier, and work up to imagining success at more difficult actions.*

Brian realizes that he was trying to imagine a successful putt that would be one of the longest putts he had ever made. He changes the image so that he is only a couple of feet from the cup. This time, it is easy to imagine the ball going into the cup. After doing this a couple of times, he begins to imagine putting from different positions on the green. If the ball does not go into the cup, then he imagines putting from a closer position. When Brian reflects on the experience after the session, he realizes that he was gradually able to imagine making longer putts. He started at two feet, and by the end of the session, he could consistently imagine making ten-foot putts.

Brian realizes that he can practice this in a brief session by imagining making just one successful putt from a close distance.

Maria's Experience with Directed Imagination

Maria has a presentation coming up in three weeks. She feels more comfortable speaking up at meetings after practicing the heightened focus application, but she knows that she won't be able to give her talk without feeling agitated. Maria also knows that giving a mock presentation can help. She realizes that she can use directed imagination to imagine giving her talk, and that this will enable her to practice it many times before she has to give it.

Maria sits down for her extended session of directed imagination, and focuses her intention to give the talk calmly and clearly. After relaxing for a couple of minutes, she imagines that she is starting her talk. She concentrates on the things that she wants to say, and imagines that she is standing in front of the audience and beginning her presentation. The image that appears is muddled. As Maria struggles to clarify it, she realizes that she is not absolutely sure of what she wants to say. This astonishes her, because she thought that she knew what points she wanted to make. She remembers, *When using directed imagination, you must have a clear idea of what you want to accomplish. This will be difficult if your idea of what you want to accomplish is vague or complex. Concentrate on what you want to accomplish until you have a clear idea of it, which may take a couple of sessions. Only after you have a clear image of success should you use directed imagination.*

Maria focuses on the ideas that she wants to present. She attends to other ideas that come to mind, continuing to do this for the next few minutes. Suddenly, she sees how some of the ideas that she wants to present do not fit in with the main point of her presentation. She also realizes that she has new ideas that will fit with the main point and demonstrate it more clearly. She reflects on this, and then gets a pen and paper to write down these new ideas. After writing them down, she starts the directed imagination exercise again. This time, she is able to get a clear image of giving the presentation. She notices that she is able to imagine delivering the points she wants to make in a clear and calm manner, without anxiety.

After giving the imagined talk, Maria reflects on her experience. She reviews the highlights of the presentation and considers how the exercise forced her to clarify her objectives. She realizes that she can do a brief version of the exercise in which she imagines delivering the main points of the talk.

INSTRUCTIONS FOR DIRECTED IMAGINATION

This technique combines concentrating, attending, and centering.

IMPORTANT: We advise you to avoid choosing goals that involve comparisons with others. For example, setting a personal record in an event is an acceptable goal; beating everyone else in the event is not. Although one can successfully visualize winning awards, we believe that caution is necessary. If two people visualize winning the same award, then conflict is inevitable. Inner peace is not found by becoming more competitive.

1. Sit or lie in a comfortable position in which you can completely relax.
2. Start by focusing your intention on achieving your goal.
3. Center on achieving the desired result or goal. This may be more of an idea than a concrete event.
4. Attend to thoughts, sensations, and emotions that arise. Make sure that you are aware of the emotions that are connected to achieving your goal. Continue this process

until you can vividly imagine the experience of achieving your goal.

5. Concentrate on that experience until you are absorbed in it. Make sure that you imagine the emotions as well as the sights, sounds, and other sensory experiences.
6. As you end your concentrating, reflect on any ideas that come to mind.
7. Develop a brief version of the exercise in which you imagine the highlights, and practice the brief version frequently each day.

Brian and Maria's Results from Directed Imagination

Brian has practiced the extended version of directed imagination for about four weeks. He can consistently imagine successful putts. He has also practiced the brief version a couple of times per day, and the combination of the two practices has caused him to imagine successful putts even while he is not thinking about golf. These will occur while he is walking or driving, or taking a shower.

The results have been pleasing. Brian's increased confidence at putting has helped him to be more relaxed during his approach shots. Because he is more relaxed on those shots, they are more accurate. His putts are more accurate as well. He has taken five strokes off his handicap in the last month.

Maria used directed imagination diligently during the three weeks before her presentation. She used the extended version twice per week, and she practiced a brief version several times each day. Within a couple of days of starting the exercise, she found that ideas for improving the talk were occurring spontaneously. She started carrying a notepad to jot them down. Her imagined presentation became clearer and more coherent.

When she gave the talk, it was much easier then usual. She was still anxious before it began, but once she started, the imagined practice sessions carried her through. She was able to make each of her points in a calm, unhurried manner. She also answered questions without getting flustered.

CLEARING BLOCKS

Goal-oriented visualization can be very useful at helping us succeed. However, sometimes we have unconscious mental blocks that get in the way of success. These blocks can be negative or positive. Negative blocks keep us from using our skills and abilities in a fulfilling manner. Such blocks are often related to unconscious fears of failure; they can also come from emotionally painful experiences. Negative blocks must be overcome so that we can move on.

It may seem strange, but sometimes blocks are good for us. Positive blocks keep us from achieving successes that we are attracted to, but which could cause trouble for us. For example, we may want to make more money, but that could harm our family relationships. Sometimes, we think we know what we want, but a deeper, inner self knows better. This inner self then puts up one obstacle after another. The goal becomes more and more difficult to reach. People often spend a great deal of energy chasing goals that they later find meaningless. Positive blocks are warnings that we are trying to go in a direction that is not good for us. They must be listened to, so that we can move in the right direction.

Clearing blocks is for people who feel that something internal is getting in the way of their success. It is also for people who may be uneasy about the goals that they are pursuing. Clearing blocks is definitely required when directed imagination does not succeed, or has only partial success.

Brian's Experience with Clearing Blocks

Brian is very pleased with how directed imagination and heightened focus have improved his golf game. He has taken five strokes off his handicap in a month. Several of his playing buddies are impressed by his improvement. He wants to keep getting better, and is thinking a lot about how he can improve even more. He is considering new golf clubs, and wants to increase his visualization practice. Golf is on his mind more than ever.

After a few days, Brian notices that he can't seem to succeed at the directed imagination exercise any more. The images waver, and he can't imagine successful putts, even if he tries making them a couple of feet from the cup. His efforts to continue the technique just seem to cause strain. When he asks his teacher about this, the response is, *It seems that your mind is telling you it doesn't want to do that technique. There may be a good reason. Practice the clearing blocks technique to find out what your mind is struggling with.*

Brian sits down for the session. He remembers his intention to improve his golf game. He imagines himself on the golf course, and after the image becomes clear, he does an opening technique. He imagines being on a high mountain, and the scene from the golf course is far below him. He feels peaceful and content as he experiences the vastness of the mountain. As he imagines the golf course far below, he remembers his intention is to improve his golf game. Brian notices that something is disturbing the peace he feels. As he attends to it, he identifies it as uneasiness, as if something is not quite right. He notices that this feeling increases if he observes the scene of the golf course. He again remembers his intention to improve his golf game.

Suddenly, Brian hears the words, "What will that get me?" As he imagines looking down on the golf course again, the words repeat: "What will that get me?" Brian sees other images coming into view. He attends to these and identifies them as his wife, his children, his house, and his job. He realizes that his golf game was becoming an obsession. If he had continued, he would have been spending more and more time and money on it. This time and money would be better used elsewhere. He realizes that continuing to focus so much energy on his golf game would have a negative impact on his job and on his family life. He knows that it is not worth it.

From his imagined position high on the mountain, Brian can see golf in perspective. It is just one part of his life, and its purpose is for him to have fun and relax. He is not a professional golfer, and he can be content with that fact. Brian feels a sense of relief, like something that was squeezing his mind has loosened its grasp. He reviews the insights he has gained from the session, and then reorients to time and place before opening his eyes.

Maria's Experience with Clearing Blocks

Maria has been pleased with the success of directed imagination. She is much less anxious when giving presentations. However, there are still occasions when she feels tension in her stomach and weakness in her legs. These occur as she starts her talk, and at random intervals during it. The episodes last only a few seconds, but they are distressing. Maria has not been able to eliminate them with directed imagination. She decides to try the clearing blocks technique.

Maria starts by focusing her intention to understand why she is still feeling bursts of anxiety when giving presentations. She focuses on the image of herself giving a talk, and she repeats her intention to herself. Maria then goes though the opening technique she enjoys, by imagining her body expanding and contracting as she breathes. She has practiced this enough that her mind responds quickly. Soon, she feels like she is drifting peacefully. *Remember your intention every now and then, to keep your mind oriented. If you just enjoy the peace, you may not get the information you want.* Maria remembers the reason that she is doing the exercises, and sees herself standing at the front of a room giving a talk. As she watches, the scene seems to get more distant, like she is floating away from it. She remembers her intention again, and the scene drifts closer. This sequence repeats itself a couple of times. Suddenly, Maria realizes that the scene has changed. As she attends to the details, she notices that she is much younger and that the room is a classroom.

Maria feels sad and anxious as she notices these details. She identifies the emotions, and disengages from them by focusing on her expansion and contraction. As Maria watches the scene, she remembers having to give an oral report in the fifth grade. She remembers getting ready to speak, and then having an attack of stage fright and forgetting everything she was going to say. It was very embarrassing. Several of her classmates laughed, and she felt like running away and never coming back. She was unable to give the report. What hurt the most was that she had worked hard on the report, but her teacher blamed her stage fright on a lack of preparation. She felt shame and hurt at her teacher's scolding. The experience had been forgotten, but the shame and hurt continued to affect her for years.

As Maria remembers all of this, the hurt and fear seem to arise and then dissipate in the spaciousness. She watches this happen, and then can remember the event without much reaction. It happened, it was uncomfortable, she was misunderstood, and now she can move beyond that. Maria reflects on this realization, and ends the session by reorienting to time and place and then opening her eyes.

INSTRUCTIONS FOR CLEARING BLOCKS

Sometimes a goal seems elusive, or it seems that something is blocking us from it. When this occurs in spite of using directed imagination, a different approach is needed.

Directed imagination uses concentrating on achieving the goal to generate a laser-like focus on success. Clearing blocks uses opening and spaciousness to pull back from the goal and to see what might be causing the difficulties.

1. Start by sitting or lying in a comfortable position.
2. Set your intention to understand what the blocks are to attaining your goal, and how to resolve them.
3. Center on the image of achieving the goal. Attend to thoughts, emotions, and sensations that arise.
4. Use an opening technique to mentally pull back from the image. For example, imagine being on a mountaintop, and see the image of the goal farther and farther below you.
5. Notice ideas or images that come to mind. Stay alert for any that seem to be opposed to achieving the goal.
6. Restate your intention a couple of times, and continue to apply the opening technique. For example, continue to imagine yourself on the mountaintop, seeing things far below you.
7. As you come out of the meditation, reflect on the ideas and images that came up, and take notes on any that seem relevant or surprising.

This exercise is essentially the opposite of directed imagination, in which you center on the goal, allow it to develop by attending, and then focus your awareness by concentrating. In clearing blocks, you center on the goal, allow it to develop by attending, and then *expand* your awareness by opening.

Brian and Maria's Results with Clearing Blocks

After practicing the clearing blocks exercise, Brian feels much less intent on improving his golf game. He continues to use the brief visualization of successful putting every now and then. He also uses the heightened focus technique when he is playing. However, he realizes that there are more important things than golf. One of the most important of these is his family. He plans to start the relationship applications of meditation in his next session.

Maria felt a real relief after practicing the clearing blocks exercise. She now feels much easier about speaking out. She no longer has anxiety attacks during presentations. All she feels is a mild discomfort as she prepares to start speaking. She realizes that this is normal performance anxiety, and it actually gets her energized so that she can deliver a good talk. She is satisfied with the results of the performance applications, and is looking forward to using the techniques for improving relationships.

CONCLUSION

You now have a set of tools that will enable you to improve your performance in a large number of activities. You will improve while keeping a sense of efficiency and flow. You will feel less need to compete, and will be able to simply act and let the results take care of themselves. This will increase your sense of peace, as you use your energy more coherently on tasks that are truly important to you.

As you practice the three applications, you will find that they complement each other. Heightened focus enhances your awareness while performing an activity, and allows you to maintain a calm attitude as well. As you practice it, you will find that it becomes effortless. That state of effortless intensity and calm is sometimes referred to as "the zone," and is associated with peak performances.

Directed imagination enables you to train your mind to experience success before an event occurs. It is important to imagine success, because you will teach your mind whatever it is that you imagine. As you get familiar with directed imagination, you will find that your mind is imagining success even while you are involved in other activities that do not absorb your attention. That is the real power of the technique. Your mind does the practice automatically, without needing your attention.

Clearing blocks keeps you from pursuing goals that are not right for you. It helps you to guide your use of directed imagination and heightened focus to activities that are best for you. Clearing blocks also helps you to overcome the inhibiting effects of negative past experiences, so that the first two exercises can work more effectively.

After you have completed this chapter and made progress toward enhancing your performance, you may be tempted to focus on another set of performance goals. However, we advise you to work on applications from another chapter. There will always be more ways to improve your performance, but a peaceful life involves more than just being good at tasks. If you skipped over the health applications, go back to them; otherwise, move on to the applications for relationships and spirituality.

ten

Relationships: creating peace at Home

It is the integration of compassion (masculine) and wisdom (feminine) that results in ultimate happiness.

Tibetan Buddhist Saying

Relationships can be a source of incredible peace and happiness. Unfortunately, they can also be a source of conflict and distress. The same relationship can be the source of both peace and conflict. If you are like everyone else we know, you would like your relationships to be more peaceful and loving.

When we think about improving relationships, most of us think we need to understand the other person. Men need to understand women, women need to understand men. Unfortunately, useful distinctions between the sexes often degenerate into stereotyping. Men are supposed to fit one pattern, women another. True communication is lost as we translate each other's words according to the formula from the latest book.

Descriptions of differences between men and women can certainly provide hints regarding the source of relationship difficulties. However, both men and women are human beings. As humans, they have certain important traits in common. These shared traits cause difficulties when men and women attempt to maintain relationships. By practicing meditation techniques that counter these traits, you will create an atmosphere that becomes a foundation for true understanding. Because these traits are shared by both men and women, when you counter their effects you will improve all your close relationships, not just those with the opposite sex.

The three applications presented in this chapter counter difficulties that we have observed in almost everyone we have worked with. Building positive energy teaches you how to increase the sense of caring and affection in your relationship, avoiding the "where's my dinner" trap. Closeness during conflict allows you to handle "hot" issues without losing touch with the other person. Space without distance allows you to experience a sense of personal space without having to become emotionally distant from your partner.

BUILDING POSITIVE ENERGY

There is a story about a young student who lived next door to a family with young children. The mother cooked for her husband and children and noticed that the student was quite poor. She felt it was little bother to cook an extra portion for dinner and have one of her children take it to the student. For the first week, the student was quite thankful for receiving this free food. As the food kept coming day after day, however, the student's thanks became less and less audible. After several weeks, the mother had a very difficult day. All her children were sick and she was unable to cook dinner. Shortly after the usual dinner time had come and gone, she heard a knock on the door. When the harried mother opened it, she saw the student standing there. "Where's my dinner?" he asked.

Many relationships have a balance of positive and negative energies. There are things we really like about the other person, and there are things we could do without. Over time, the positive things are taken more and more for granted. They become less noticeable. Or, they are noticed only when they are suddenly not there, like the student's dinner. As the positive elements of the relationship become less noticeable, the negative ones loom larger. Usually, they are not really growing. The problem is that the positive side of the relationship has gradually become invisible.

Building positive energy is a meditation technique that restores your awareness of the positive side to your relationships. To do the exercise, you center on the positive side of the relationship by thinking about the kind and loving things the other person does for you. Sometimes the positive side is small and flickering. But even the embers of a loving relationship can be rekindled by reminding yourself of the positive things that are present.

Brian's Experience with Building Positive Energy

Brian begins his morning meditation session with the intention to improve his relationship with his teenage son. They quarrel often, and it seems that they are always finding fault with each other. He has noticed some improvement since he began meditating several months ago. He would like to continue improving the relationship and do it more rapidly. He focuses his intention by thinking about this for a couple of minutes. Brian then centers on the sensations in his lower abdomen as he thinks "calm—relaxed" several times. After a few breaths he feels the familiar sense of calm. Brian then centers on positive memories of his son, by thinking about some good things that his son has done and the positive feelings associated with them. As he does this, he starts to remember numerous negative things. His son's report card, messy room, clothing and hair styles, and loud obnoxious music come to mind. He identifies these and disengages from them, deliberately returning to centering on the positive things his son has done.

However, Brian's irritation quickly returns. The memories of what he doesn't like about his son's behavior are entangling his mind. Brian struggles to return to his desired center, the positive memories, but he cannot. *Sometimes you will get caught by negative memories, and you won't be able to go directly back to the positive memories. When this happens, identify the emotions that you are feeling, and ignore the specific memories. Then go back to centering on your breath until you have disengaged from those negative emotions. Once you have done so, you are ready to return to centering on the positive memories.*

Brian identifies his emotions as anger and frustration. He then centers on the sensations in his lower abdomen, and disengages from the emotions. The negative memories recede and, after a few breaths, he is able to think again about the positive aspects of his relationship with his son.

He notes that there are times when his son does speak respectfully to him. His son has also thanked him on a number of occasions. While his son's report card was not as good as Brian wanted it to be, there were a number of good grades on it.

When the session is over, Brian reflects on his experience. He realizes that there were a number of positive things he remembered during the exercise that he hadn't before. He realizes that this will help him keep a more balanced perspective on how his son is actually doing.

Maria's Experience with Building Positive Energy

Maria has decided to spend some focused meditation time on improving the relationship she has with her husband. He has complained frequently about being nagged by her. As her self-awareness has increased since she began meditating, she has noticed that she does complain frequently. Her meditation practice has helped her reduce her complaints, but she feels that she needs to do something more definite about the problem.

Maria focuses her intention to improve the relationship, and specifically to center on the positive aspects of it during this session. Because she feels a little tense, she does the autonomic relaxation exercise for a couple of minutes, ending with the phrase, "my face is soft and smiling." She then begins to think about the things her husband has done that are nice. At first she draws a blank, and thinks, "But he hasn't done anything really nice." She remembers her teacher's advice: *When you look for positive things about your husband to center on, look for little things. Remember any smiles, any caresses, any times he did something helpful around the house. Think about how much effort he puts into the family. By focusing on the little things, you will reinforce the positive, and that will lead to bigger things.*

Maria stays relaxed and begins to remember things her husband has done to help out with the children. She then remembers several times when he helped out with dinner, or with cleaning up afterward. She sees him playing with the children on weekends, and giving her the time to meditate after work. She then remembers how often he does smile at her, and how often he is affectionate. The exercise seems to flow easily, and she is surprised by how easy it is to center on the positive feelings, and remember the good times.

When the session ends, Maria reflects on the experience. She realizes that she and her husband have a lot of love and caring in their relationship. She also notes that she often complains, not because her husband hasn't helped, but because he hasn't helped in exactly the way she wanted him to. Maria decides that demanding he do things just the way she wants is a little unfair, and that she can show him more appreciation for what he does.

INSTRUCTIONS FOR BUILDING POSITIVE ENERGY

1. Focus your intention to center on the positive aspects of the relationship by thinking about the good things in it.
2. If you are feeling tense, do a calming exercise for a couple of minutes.
3. Remember any actions the other person did that were kind and loving. Center on the positive side of the relationship by returning your awareness to such memories.
4. If negative thoughts or memories should come up, identify them and disengage from them by remembering the positive ones.
5. If you get caught by negative memories, disengage by identifying the emotions associated with them, and then center on something physical like the sensations in your lower abdomen, or the sensations of air moving in and out of your nose. When you feel calm, go back to centering on the positive things in the relationship.
6. At the end of the session, reflect on your experience, especially noting any positive things that you hadn't remembered before. Also note any patterns in the distracting thoughts or sensations.

Brian and Maria's Results from Building Positive Energy

After one week of practicing building positive energy, Brian is able to do it more easily. The negative thoughts that were upsetting him are much weaker. He has reflected that his irritation about how his son dresses and keeps his room is ironic, as these are things that irritated Brian's parents when he was a child. He still wants his son to improve, but he realizes that improvement will be more likely if he reinforces the positive behaviors instead of just criticizing the negative ones.

Maria has practiced building positive energy for a week. She feels her emotions toward her husband becoming steadier, more consistently warm. She finds it easier to show appreciation for the positive things he does. This is making the atmosphere around the house much warmer. He is also being more receptive to her when she does complain.

CLOSENESS DURING CONFLICT

Conflict will arise eventually in every one of your relationships. To have successful relationships, you must be able to resolve conflicts. In our experience, most people avoid conflict because it makes them uncomfortable. If the problem were discussed, strong negative emotions might be triggered, buttons could be pushed, and so the issue is avoided. No one wants to rock the boat. Of course, this doesn't resolve the problem; the "hot issue" is not discussed, and this leads to a cold war.

Fortunately, the meditation techniques that you have learned can be used to make it easier for you to resolve conflicts. As we discussed in the chapter on performance, your mind doesn't distinguish between a vividly imagined event and a real event. You can use meditation to practice keeping your negative emotions under control while in conflict. You can identify buttons before they are pushed, and desensitize yourself to them. After you have practiced this in meditation, it is much safer to address the issue with the other person.

This exercise has an added benefit: often, the problem issue is associated with other fears or irritations that you have about the relationship, which are hiding from you. This practice can make you aware of those hidden issues, and help you see clearly what really needs to be addressed when you talk with the other person.

You will get better results with this exercise if you have practiced building positive energy for a couple of weeks before starting this one. That way, you will have reinforced your awareness of how much love and caring there is in the relationship, before you start to work on issues.

Brian's Experience with Closeness during Conflict

Brian and his wife consistently argue about money. He gets upset about the amount that she spends, but whenever they try to talk about it, they have an argument or even a verbal fight. He will become loud and accusatory, and she will get hurt and become sullen. This causes a bad feeling between them that can last for days. The subject of money has become so hot that Brian does not even bring it up. He just tries to put it out of his mind.

Brian is going to use closeness during conflict to help him talk reasonably about some of their financial issues, without getting so upset that it leads to a fight. He knows that this is an emotional subject, so he figures that he will have to spend several sessions on it.

After Brian focuses on his intention of being able to talk calmly about finances, he remembers an important point from his teacher. *Make sure that you center on something calming at the beginning of the exercise. Then, if you experience intense emotions, you can recenter on that to calm yourself.* As Brian sits quietly, he centers on the thoughts "calm" as he inhales and "relaxed" as he exhales. Once he is relaxed, he thinks about the last credit card bill that he saw. He remembers that it was higher than he had expected, and that he had become upset about it. As he remembers this, he feels a tightness in his stomach, and tension in his jaw and throat. He identifies these sensations, disengages from them, and concentrates again on the memory of the credit card bill.

Brian then identifies a number of familiar thoughts. "She's always spending money . . . Why does she have to buy everything she sees?" Brian identifies these thoughts, but can't disengage from them and go back to remembering the credit card bill. He is too upset. *When you are unable to disengage from negative thoughts, identify the emotion behind those thoughts, and disengage from it by centering on something calming until you feel peaceful.* Brian identifies the emotion that is associated with those thoughts as anger, and disengages from it by centering on the thoughts "calm—relaxed." After a minute or so, Brian feels calmer and is able to remember the credit card bill again.

Brian has to repeat this several times, but each time it is easier to disengage from his anger. Then, as he is remembering the credit card bill, he notices that he is also thinking about what his wife has bought for their children. He identifies this thought, and then notices that he feels somewhat pleased. This emotion surprises him, but he identifies it and goes back to remembering the bill.

Suddenly, Brian feels like a door has opened up in his mind, and a large number of memories, thoughts, and emotions pours through. He remembers being a child and wanting clothes that his family was too poor to buy. He thinks about the clothes, and about gifts that he wishes he could buy for his children. He thinks about the vacations he would like to take with his wife, but which they can't afford. He wonders if he is really providing enough for his family. He wonders if his wife is really satisfied with him. He feels despondent and inadequate.

Brian is shocked by the intensity of his experience. He feels almost drowned by the flood of emotion that has poured in. He hears the voice of his teacher faintly, *This exercise can bring up strong emotions. Remember your anchor, remember to center on what calms you until you can disengage from the emotions.* Brian focuses his awareness on the sensations in his abdomen and thinks "calm" as he inhales and "relaxed" as he exhales. His months of practice have made this a powerful calming anchor for him. He feels the emotions of sadness and inadequacy fade, and feels his body relax.

Brian feels exhausted, and realizes that he must stop the exercise. As he reflects on the experience, he realizes that the issue is not really how much his wife is spending. The hidden problem is his fear that she does not think he is a good provider. He also realizes that he will need to repeat this exercise several more times before he will be able to talk coherently with his wife about this issue.

Maria's Experience with Closeness during Conflict

Maria has the impression that she is fighting with her children almost constantly about the messes they make. It seems that she is scolding them every day. She knows that she is overreacting to what is rather normal behavior for young children, but she can't seem to stop herself.

As Maria starts her first session of closeness during conflict, she remembers, *After focusing your intention, center on something calming that can serve as an anchor if you experience intense feelings.* Maria thinks about her desire to respond more constructively to the messes her children make. She then centers on the phrase "my face is soft and smiling." She has been using that as a brief relaxation technique for several weeks, and it has a strong calming effect on her.

After a few seconds, Maria feels relaxed, and she concentrates on the last time she found her children's books and toys scattered over the living room after she had told them to clean up. Immediately, her body tenses, and she feels angry. She identifies the tension and anger and disengages from them, going back to the memory of the messy room. The anger returns, and she also has the thought that her children are ignoring her. This thought intensifies her anger. Maria identifies the thought and the anger and tries to disengage from them, but cannot. She focuses on the phrase "my face is soft and smiling," but notices that her face feels hard and angry. *If focusing on something calming does not work, then focus on a positive aspect of the relationship with the person you are having difficulty with.* Maria remembers some of the cute things her children have done. As she concentrates on those memories, she feels her anger subside.

Maria then goes back to concentrating on the memory of the messy room. This time she feels frustration. The thought associated with the frustration is that she has told her children repeatedly to clean up with no results. Maria identifies the frustration and associated thought, and disengages from them by refocusing on the positive memories of her children. Maria repeats this process of switching between the memory of the messy room, identifying the thoughts and emotions that are evoked, and disengaging from them by remembering positive scenes with her children.

After several repetitions, Maria realizes that she is feeling fear. As she identifies this emotion, she realizes that she is thinking that her children have no discipline. She is afraid that they will grow up to be irresponsible; that they will become delinquents or derelicts. Maria is shocked by these fearful thoughts. She identifies them and disengages from them, focusing on the positive memories. Maria then realizes how silly these fears are. Her children are well-behaved most of the time, and hardly act like delinquents. Maria feels a sense of relief, and realizes that now her face is soft and smiling.

Maria refocuses on the memory of the messy room, and soon has the insight that her children might feel overwhelmed by her demand that they clean it unassisted. As she realizes this, her alarm beeps, signaling the end of the session. Maria finishes the exercise by reflecting on her new insights. She observes that she needs to get rid of the illogical fear that her children will grow up to be delinquents, which is fueling much of her anger and frustration. She also reflects that she will have to try a different approach to getting them to clean their messes.

INSTRUCTIONS FOR CLOSENESS DURING CONFLICT

1. Sit or lie down in a comfortable position in which you can completely relax.
2. Focus your intention to be able to be in conflict with your partner while staying calm and maintaining a sense of respect and connection.
3. Center on a calming sensation or image. This will be an anchor throughout the exercise.

4. Once you are calm, concentrate on the issue that you are in conflict about. You can often do this by concentrating on the memory of an event in which the other person did something to upset you (or didn't do something you wanted). Focus on what the other person did or said.
5. Attend to thoughts, sensations, and emotions that come up (that is, identify them and disengage from them). If you start to feel too tense or agitated, go back to centering on the calming sensation or image. If that doesn't work, focus on a positive memory about the person. IMPORTANT: As you identify thoughts, sensations, and emotions, pay particular attention to those that seem new to you, or those that seem deeper than the usual thoughts you have about the issue. Remain calm while you imagine the conflict and attend to the thoughts, and so forth, that arise.
6. As you end your concentrating, reflect on any ideas that come to mind. Be especially aware of any ideas that seem to give you a different perspective on the conflict.
7. Practice until you can remain calm throughout the exercise, and have a sense that you can really experience your partner's perspective.

Brian and Maria's Results with Closeness during Conflict

Brian had to practice closeness during conflict several times before he could stay calm during the exercise. He realized that the financial issues would not be resolved overnight, but he knew that he could stay calmer during a discussion. He also recognized that his sadness (at not having all the money he wanted to buy things for his family) was what triggered his angry reaction.

Brian talked with his wife about guidelines for discussing finances together. He told her that he gets tense because he wishes he made more money than he does, which was not her fault. He said that if he got tense during a discussion he would ask for a "time-out" for a few minutes, so he could calm himself. He also asked her to try to avoid being critical of how much money he made, as that would fuel his sadness and frustration. His wife agreed to work within those rules. She also reassured him that she was quite satisfied with his income, and that she was grateful that he was working on improving their relationship. Their next discussion about bills was difficult and he had to take several time-outs, but it was also more constructive and there was no anger or bitterness afterward.

Maria practiced closeness during conflict once more, concentrating on the messes her children make. It was much easier to stay calm in the second session, and she realized that if her children were really feeling overwhelmed by her demands that they clean up, then she needed to act differently. She decided to change her approach by helping them start cleaning their mess. This required her to participate for most of the cleaning-up the first couple of times, but it still took less time and energy on her part then her former practice of yelling. After she had helped them clean their mess a few times, she noticed that her children required less participation on her part and were doing more of the work themselves. They still seemed to want her to be present for most of the cleaning-up, but she was able to relax during the process and even find it enjoyable. Once, after cleaning up their mess with her, the children followed her around the house helping her with the rest of the cleaning. Their help did not speed things up greatly, but it was fun and it put to rest Maria's fears that her children were irresponsible.

SPACE WITHOUT DISTANCE

Many times, we feel crowded in a relationship. As much as we love the people around us, we feel as if they are too close—we want space. This need for space is important and often healthy. It is a sign that we want to grow, to explore other aspects of our lives. Problems result because most people equate space with distance. When they want space, they feel that they need to become more distant from the people around them. Sometimes this actually causes a person to create conflict, to make others back off in order to satisfy the need for space.

However, the space that we want in a relationship is psychological space. For the mind, space and distance need not be the same. Remember that spaciousness is a natural mental quality. Your mind has all the space it needs. When you know how to experience that space, you do not need to become more distant from the ones you love.

Imagine that you and the other people in your life were living on a flat surface, with no idea of the space above or below you. Then it would be natural to feel crowded when they got close to you. Now, imagine that you discovered all the room above and below you. You would suddenly experience plenty of space, without having to move away from anyone. In fact, you could even get closer to others and still feel that you had plenty of space.

Practicing space without distance does this for you. You will experience having the space to grow and change, without having to distance yourself from those you love. The exercise uses your mind's natural quality of spaciousness, and allows you to be creative so that you can meet your needs for space and still maintain closeness.

Brian's Experience with Space without Distance

Brian is able to talk about money and other issues with his wife more easily now, and this has eased the tension in their relationship. However, one continuing source of difficulty is what happens when Brian is feeling stressed and wants to be alone. His wife seems to sense that something is wrong, and asks him questions. These increase his stress, because he knows his desire to withdraw and be alone is upsetting his wife. He becomes even more quiet and distant. Then his wife gets visibly upset and accuses him of not talking, of not sharing his feelings. When he hears that, Brian gets so upset that he often has to leave the house for a while.

Brian is hopeful about practicing space without distance. He thinks that if he can learn to feel space without making his wife feel distance, then they will be more comfortable. Brian sits down to practice, and begins by focusing his intention to feel the space he needs while staying emotionally close to his wife. He goes quickly through the autonomic relaxation exercise to relax deeply.

Brian then thinks about the warmth and love he and his wife have for each other. He quickly feels the positive emotions he has toward her. He then does the opening technique of imagining that he is on a mountaintop. He experiences the vastness and feels as if there is an immense space about him.

Within a couple of minutes, Brian feels like he is high above things. The air is clear and crisp, and it is very quiet. He watches the things he is stressed about get more distant. He then recalls the warm feelings he has for his wife. He imagines that she is sitting near him on the mountaintop, not crowding him, but just present. He can still feel the space above, around, and below him.

As Brian does this, he sees images of the things that cause him stress: his job, worries about the economy, worries about his kids. He focuses more strongly on the sense of vastness and allows these images to move farther away. At the same time, he thinks again about the positive feelings he has for his wife. Her image stays close and the stressful images move off into the distance.

Brian is enjoying this process. He is experiencing the warmth, love, and presence of his partner, while separating from the stresses that cause him to shut down. He realizes that he can feel comfortable with her presence if she is willing to sit more quietly and ask fewer questions. He reflects on this new insight and realizes he has never tried just sitting quietly and lovingly with his wife. He decides that this will be worth attempting. He then reorients to the time and place, flexes his arms and legs, and opens his eyes.

Maria's Experience with Space without Distance

Maria has been pleased with the results of closeness during conflict. She is handling her children's messes without yelling or nagging. However, there are still times when she feels irritated by the disorder around the house, and not just because of her children's messes. Her husband will leave his clothes lying around, or throw his jacket over a chair when he comes home from work. These things sometimes make Maria wish that she lived by herself, so that everything would stay in its proper place. It is then that she feels annoyed and acts irritably.

Maria decides to use space without distance to reduce her sensitivity to some of the normal disorder in the household. She starts by focusing her intention to be at ease and feel like she has her own space, in spite of the presence of the other people at home.

Maria relaxes, and then remembers some of the things that she enjoys about her family members. She concentrates on the positive feelings generated by those memories. She experiences the love and caring that she has for her husband and children.

Maria then uses the opening technique that she has had success with before. She focuses on the experience of her body expanding as she inhales and contracting as she exhales. Soon, she feels the familiar sense of drifting. She continues to bring the positive memories of her family to mind while she drifts comfortably. She begins to see many other scenes from family life flowing into one another. She feels that she is still herself, even though her husband and children influence her. As she enjoys the floating sensations, she experiences a whole new dimension of her being that is free. It is not hindered by the needs and actions of her family members. Her mind relaxes even more, and even the images fade into a comfortable sense of peacefulness.

Maria enjoys the experience, and when her alarm beeps, she reflects on how she needs to separate who she is from what she does. She picks up after her children and occasionally after her husband, but that is not who she is. She is a not a maid, even if she has to clean up at times.

INSTRUCTIONS FOR SPACE WITHOUT DISTANCE

1. Start by sitting or lying in a comfortable position.
2. Focus your intention to experience a sense of personal space while staying close to your partner.
3. Center on a positive memory of your partner. Attend to the thoughts, emotions, and sensations that arise. Concentrate on the positive feeling that you have for your partner.

4. Use an opening technique to experience a sense of vastness, while staying connected to the positive feeling. For example, imagine being on a mountaintop and see the image of your partner at a comfortable distance.
5. Continue to remind yourself of the positive feelings as well as the vastness, until you experience a sense of space as well as the positive feelings. While experiencing the sense of space, attend to thoughts, images, and ideas that come to mind.
6. As you come out of the meditation, reflect on the ideas and images that came up, and take notes on any that seem relevant or surprising.

This exercise brings creativity into our relationships, helping us to resolve our need for growth as an individual while still maintaining emotional closeness.

Brian and Maria's Results with Space without Distance

Several days after the space without distance session, Brian comes home from work stressed out. He feels the familiar desire to be silent and withdraw. His wife seems to sense this, and asks the usual question, "What's wrong?" Just as Brian starts to answer with "Nothing," he catches himself. Instead, he asks, "Do you have a few minutes?" His wife seems surprised by the question, but answers, "Yes." Luckily, the house is quiet, and they sit down together on the couch. Brian says, "I'm OK, I don't need to talk. But I do want to sit close to you for a few minutes." He puts his arm around her, and she leans up against him.

Brian closes his eyes and remembers the experience from the session of space without distance. He can feel the pleasant warmth of his wife's body against his. He imagines being on the mountaintop with all the pressures and worries of the day falling off into the distance. He connects more strongly with the presence of his wife. He can feel the freedom of the space and the comfortable warmth of her next to him. He feels his whole body relax; as he does, he feels his wife relax also. They sit together for a few more minutes, and then Brian says, "You know, I love you and I'm really glad you're here." His wife responds with a warm hug and they get up together.

Brian realizes that he doesn't feel as withdrawn now. While he still wants some time by himself, he feels comfortably connected to his wife. His wife also seems to be more comfortable. She is not pursuing him with questions, and the evening passes peacefully.

One evening, after Maria had practiced space without distance a couple of times, her husband came home and left his coat draped over the living room chair. Maria was about to make a sharp retort when she remembered her experiences from the space without distance exercise. Feeling a need for space at the moment, she took a deep breath and imagined space filling her whole body. Then she exhaled and imagined plenty of space around her, and especially between her and the coat on the chair.

Maria felt her mind clear, and she noticed that her husband looked a little upset. She asked him if he wanted some quiet time, or if he wanted to go for a little walk. He looked a little surprised, and agreed that a short walk would be nice. He picked up his jacket, put it back on, and headed out the door. A short time later, he returned. His mood was lighter, and when he took off his jacket he hung it up in the closet. Maria smiled to herself. She had used much less energy and gotten better results than if she had reacted in her usual manner

CONCLUSION

Having peaceful relationships with a partner, family members, or others, helps you to maintain a sense of inner peace. You need more than the absence of fighting to have a peaceful relationship. You must experience the relationship as being positive and caring, and must be able to resolve difficult issues instead of having to avoid them. Finally, you must be able to grow personally while staying connected to the other person.

The three applications of meditation in this chapter counter common tendencies that disrupt the positive interactions in a relationship. By practicing them, you will be able to improve your relationship with your partner. You will also be able to improve relationships with your children, friends, and colleagues at work.

Like the applications in the preceding chapters, these three applications are best practiced in sequence. Building positive energy will create a more positive atmosphere in the relationship. It is an antidote to the tendency for people to take positive things for granted. Building positive energy generates results quickly; people often experience a change in attitude after only one or two sessions.

Closeness during conflict is an important exercise because it enables you to practice working through a hot issue before you actually talk about it. It enables you to break the common pattern of avoiding discussions about difficult topics. Because closeness during conflict can bring up many negative feelings, it is helpful to have practiced building positive energy first. This will keep you from being overwhelmed by negative emotions when you do the exercise.

Space without distance helps resolve the paradox of needing to obtain a sense of freedom and space while remaining emotionally close to your partner. It brings creativity into the relationship, which allows you to come up with new responses to old situations. You will get better results using space without distance if you are familiar with the two previous exercises.

After you have had experience with all three applications, we recommend that you practice building positive energy for a couple of minutes at least once per day. If you are working on your relationship with a partner, one good time to use it is before returning home from work, or before your partner returns home.

You should use closeness during conflict to help you talk through specific issues. If you are enjoying a time when there seem to be no specific difficulties in the relationship, then you may not need to practice this application.

Use space without distance when you feel a need for personal space or sense a need for personal growth. Again, there may be times when you do not need this technique.

eleven

spirituality: Living with Love

Love is the seed for a bountiful crop.
Like water, love makes that crop grow,
And much later it ripens into the thing most desired.
That is why at the outset, I praise love.

Chandrakirti

Spirituality refers to the quality of our relationship to transcendence and love. The amount of peace in your life is directly related to your ability to connect with love. Your health, your performance, and even your personal relationships are all somewhat out of your control. The aspect of your life that you have the most influence over is your experience of love.

Every now and then, we have experiences of transcendence and love that break into the daily routine. These experiences are rare, and usually fleeting. Then, ordinary reality returns. We can improve our spirituality so that we experience that transcendent love on a daily, even a constant basis. Meditation was developed by spiritual traditions in order to make the experience of transcendence and love accessible and even continuous.

Because we are writing for a wide audience we will use the word "love" to indicate the presence or the idea of what people variously may call God, Jesus, "universal consciousness," or any number of other words. When we use the word "love," we mean an unconditional love and compassion that is beyond any conceptual definition. Any true experience of it defies description. Feel free to substitute your own word in place of "love," as long as the ideas of love and transcendence are present.

Meditation is a practical and rapid way to increase the experience of love in your life. Many people have difficulty believing that spiritual techniques can be so ordinary. People make them harder than they really are. The techniques we describe are practical and simple. They are within your capabilities, and are not meant for a spiritual elite. All that you need is familiarity with the basic techniques described in part I, and the willingness to be persistent in practice.

We describe three techniques for increasing the experience of love in your life. We begin with a simple technique and move to more complex ones. The most important result of practice is that you will experience love, not just while you are meditating, but more and more spontaneously throughout the day.

CENTERING PRAYER

One way to experience love in meditation is to stop and sit quietly. The presence of love is always there. Instead of being noisy and chattering away about the presence of love, or running around trying to find it somewhere, we need to place ourselves in a receptive state of mind, and listen. This is what you will do in centering prayer. It is not passive, because you must use some energy to keep yourself quiet and receptive. But neither is it active or seeking. You will exert mental energy to stay in a receptive and quiet attitude, and then wait and listen.

This method of prayer uses centering and attending skills. In order to move into a state that is receptive to the presence of love, you center on the idea of love. You then use attending skills to listen, and to disengage from any distractions. The result is an experience of inner quiet and connection with a loving presence. Mental noise gets fainter and matters less. You feel as if you are where you have been trying to get all along.

Centering on the idea of love requires some skill and practice. The idea of love is more abstract than physical sensations, images of health or performance, and feelings toward another person. The applications in the earlier chapters will have helped your mind become more comfortable centering on abstract ideas.

To center on the idea of love, spend some time thinking about what transcendent love means to you. Think about love, and how it is expressed in your life and in the world. Think about the things associated with love: caring, peace, joy, and humor. You might find yourself thinking that love can exist as a being (God), or you might simply find yourself thinking of qualities associated with love. After thinking about love for a little bit, choose one word that best represents the idea of love to you. Love, peace, joy, God, Jesus, Buddha, hope, wonder, Divine Mother or Father, consciousness, and One, are examples of words that are commonly used.

It is important that you think about transcendent love before choosing your word. That is what will give the word meaning for you; it becomes a sacred word. Once you have chosen a sacred word, then you can use the word as an anchor to help you center on the presence of love.

After you have chosen your word, you are ready to begin centering prayer. During the time of prayer, you will use the word you have chosen to help you disengage from any thoughts or sensations that distract you from the presence of love. Even thoughts about love can be distractions, so when your mind gets noisy, identify the noise and then mentally repeat your word, to help you disengage from the distraction.

Brian's Experience with Centering Prayer

Brian has thought about transcendent love for a few days. The word that has kept coming to mind has been "peace." He has decided to use that as his sacred word.

As he sits down for his morning meditation session, he focuses his intention to sit quietly and be receptive to love and peace. He then spends a couple of minutes centering on his breath, until he feels relaxed. Then he thinks the word "peace," and lets his mind reflect on the idea of peace and love. He notices a lot of thoughts about love and peace. Then he finds he is thinking about some of the negative things that go on in the world. He identifies these thoughts as negative distractions, and disengages from them by thinking "peace" several times. The negative thoughts subside and he feels a sense of quiet followed almost immediately by thoughts about love. The thoughts seem attractive and he starts to explore them. *Thoughts about love can become distracting, too. If they arise, just identify them, and disengage from them by thinking your sacred word.* Brian does this, and the sense of quiet returns. Various other thoughts arise, and he disengages from them easily. However, his mind seems to want to keep thinking actively about love and peace. *Staying quiet and receptive is difficult for people who analyze and think a lot. Being receptive is an activity that they are not used to. By disengaging from the thoughts about love, you will experience a deeper connection with love. The thoughts will return after the session. You are not banishing them forever, so sometimes telling them "later" is helpful.*

Brian thanks his mind for thinking such positive thoughts, but then tells it "later," and repeats his sacred word, "peace," gently to himself several times. Again, the sense of quiet returns and he feels as if something has joined him. He continues to sit quietly, enjoying the experience of peace until the session ends.

He then reflects on his experience, and notes how centering prayer and thinking about love are quite different. He realizes that he will have to practice stopping his tendency to analyze. He also notes that he is now having several thoughts about peace and love that are new to him.

Maria's Experience with Centering Prayer

Maria is excited about using meditation for spirituality. She spends some time thinking about love. This is surprisingly difficult for her. She felt sure that she would use "God" as her sacred word, but when she starts thinking about God as love, she realizes that God is just a word for her, and is not very connected to a deep experience of love. After spending some days reflecting on love and on her understanding of God's love for her, she feels more of a connection between the word "God" and the deep love behind it. "God" is now a sacred word for her.

Maria begins her session of centering prayer by focusing on her intention to sit quietly in the presence of a loving God. She gently repeats the word "God" to herself with every exhalation, becoming more and more relaxed. After a few minutes, her body settles and her mind becomes more quiet.

She has a series of thoughts about work and her family, but she is able to identify these and disengage from them easily. When she catches herself thinking about something, she identifies the thought and disengages from it by thinking "God" to herself. Soon she feels quite peaceful, as if she is sitting comfortably with a loving friend. Suddenly, she thinks, "Is this all there is to it? Maybe I should be doing something else?" She starts to worry, but remembers, *When you are centered in the presence of love, everything gets quiet and there is nothing more to do. Simply stay in that presence, and if something distracts you, disengage from it using your sacred word.*

Maria feels reassured, and is able to disengage from the worry and go back to enjoying the experience. Then she starts to worry again. She remembers some things that she has done that were not nice, like snapping at her husband and children. The thought comes, "You don't deserve this, you aren't good enough for it." *When you start to enjoy centering prayer, you may feel that you don't deserve the experience. That's true, in the sense that no one does, but you must accept it as a gift, and realize that practicing centering prayer will help you to become a better person. Identify such thoughts or feelings as accusations, and disengage from them using your sacred word. You are loved, even with your imperfections. If you have difficulty disengaging, simply think "I'm sorry" to help yourself disengage.*

Maria acknowledges the thoughts and identifies them as accusations. She thinks, "I apologize," and then repeats "God" several times to herself until she is disengaged from them. The rest of her meditation session consists of periods of quiet loving presence and occasional distracting thoughts. It feels quite restful. When her session ends and she reflects on the experience, she realizes that her mind was much quieter than usual. She feels a sense of inner peace and satisfaction, as though everything were taken care of and there was no need for her to do anything.

INSTRUCTIONS FOR CENTERING PRAYER

This is a basic form of contemplative prayer that is used in a number of spiritual traditions. The point is to center on the idea of love. The mind centers on an idea, not on an image or a mantram.

1. Pick a word that symbolizes the concept or presence of love to you. The word must be meaningful to you; it becomes your sacred word. Use the same word from session to session.
2. Focus on your intention to center your mind on the idea of love.
3. Mentally repeat the sacred word to yourself several times. Allow your mind to center on the idea symbolized by the word. Once your mind is connected with the idea, let go of repeating the word.
4. As long as your mind is quiet, just rest. If you get distracted, then repeat your sacred word to yourself until your mind quiets again.

After the session, recall your experience and note any patterns in the distracting thoughts or sensations.

Brian and Maria's Results from Centering Prayer

Brian has been practicing centering prayer for one month. He does it three times per week, and alternates the basic techniques of attending, concentrating, and opening in his other three weekly practice sessions. Brian finds centering prayer enjoyable. He is able to achieve inner quiet and peace within a few minutes; then he just rests there. One of the results is that he feels like he is a naturally peaceful person. Previously, he had considered himself rather tough and aggressive; now he senses that the toughness is exterior, and that underneath he is quite peaceful. He can use the toughness if he has to, but it is not who he is. This allows him to express his natural peace more easily.

Maria has found centering prayer to be very quieting. This experience of deep quiet has helped her feel less urgency during the day. She has a sense that things will work out, and that she does not need to be chronically hurried.

While Maria enjoys centering prayer, she also feels a little bored. She wants to do more than just be quiet with God. When she queried her teacher about this, he responded, *People with active minds often find centering prayer to be too quiet. It is an important technique to start with, but you will need to move to a practice that requires more mental activity.*

PRACTICING THE PRESENCE OF LOVE

Centering prayer is a good foundation for using meditation in prayer, but many people, like Maria, want to be more mentally active during prayer. They also want something that they can use throughout the day.

Practicing the presence of love meets those needs. Whereas centering prayer gives the experience of the presence of love during quiet and stillness, practicing the presence of love makes the experience of love more definite. It also strengthens the connection with love, so that the experience is available throughout the day, even during noisy or chaotic situations.

You start this technique by concentrating on the idea that love is within you and surrounding you. While you concentrate on that idea, you attend to thoughts, images, sensations, and emotions that arise. Disengage from things that distract you from the idea of love being within you and around you. However, use the clarity that comes from concentrating to stabilize the thoughts, images, and emotions that are related to the idea of love. As you do this, you will create a gradually more vivid experience of love being within you and around you. You then maintain that experience by continuing to concentrate on it for as long as is comfortable.

Practicing the presence of love is done in both extended and brief sessions. The extended sessions build a strong, tangible connection with love by using a combination of attending and concentrating skills. The brief sessions enable you to restore that connection instantly, no matter where you are, and no matter what is happening around you.

Brian's Experience with Practicing the Presence of Love

Brian starts his session of practicing the presence of love by focusing his intention to experience peace as a presence both within and around himself. He concentrates on the idea of peace being inside as well as outside of him. His mind is somewhat noisy, and he identifies the random thoughts, sensations, and emotions that appear. He is able to disengage from these just by recalling his concentration on the idea of peace inside and around himself. After a short time, his mind gets quiet and he feels peaceful inside himself.

Brian is still not aware of a sense of peace outside of himself; it all seems to be within. As he concentrates on the idea of peace surrounding him, an image starts to appear in his mind. As he attends to it, he notices that it is a figure of a monk wearing a hooded robe. He cannot see the monk's face, just the outline of the hooded robe. An aura of peace seems to flow from the monk and surround Brian. He then feels that peace flow inside him and resonate with the peace he already was feeling inside. Brian is startled, and wonders if he should disengage from this image. *If an image or thought comes to mind that increases your experience of peace, then just be aware of it. You need not disengage from it. Experience its presence and the increased peace it brings. If it fades on its own, let it go, but you need not disengage from it.*

Brian observes the image, and experiences the sense of peace filling him and surrounding him. The image fades after a few minutes, and he returns to identifying and disengaging from random mental noise. As he reflects on the experience at the end of the session, he has a vivid memory of the monk's image, and feels the peaceful aura of that figure. He remembers, *Pick a mental or physical cue that connects you with the experience, and that you can use frequently during the day.* Brian decides that the image of the monk can be a mental cue to remind him of the experience of peace.

Maria's Experience with Practicing the Presence of Love

Maria has wanted to become more active in applying meditation to spirituality. She is hoping that practicing the presence of love will satisfy her desire. Maria sits down for her meditation session, and focuses her intention to feel the presence of God within and around herself. Maria then does her usual relaxation technique of centering on the phrase "my face is soft and smiling" for a couple of minutes. This gets her into a calm and comfortable state, and then she concentrates on the idea of God being around her and within her.

Maria has the intellectual understanding that God is everywhere, but when she concentrates on the idea, she realizes that she has little emotional experience of it. *We often find that we have little real experience of the presence of love. Simply concentrate on the idea of love, and wait expectantly for images to arise. This is similar to what you do in the basic concentrating technique. Attend to images, thoughts, or feelings that come up, and disengage from those that are not helpful. Focus on those that are helpful.*

Maria waits expectantly, concentrating on the idea of God being around her and inside her. After a number of random thoughts that she disengages from, the idea of patience and understanding arises. It is as if there is a presence around her that understands her intimately, and has infinite patience with her. As she attends to this presence, she has the sense that it is feminine, like a mother who is cradling her. At first, Maria wants to reject the experience of God being feminine. Her Christian teachers usually talked about God in masculine terms, but she remembers a comment from her meditation teacher, *People are often surprised to learn that God is described in feminine terms many times in the Bible. For example, the prophet Isaiah describes God as nursing Israel—hardly a masculine activity.*

Maria relaxes, and concentrates on the feeling of being cradled by this understanding and patient presence. As she rests in the experience, she senses her own patience and understanding. She often criticizes herself for not being patient, but she now experiences that she really is a patient and understanding person. She has just not allowed these qualities to show. Maria enjoys this feeling of patience and understanding inside her. She also feels safe and loved in the arms of this motherly presence.

As she rests there, Maria remembers events in which she was patient, and others in which she was not so patient. She senses that the presence surrounding her understands that she tries, and is patient with her. Maria realizes that she needs to be more patient with herself, as well as with others.

As she finishes the exercise by reflecting on the experience, Maria decides that the cue for recalling this presence of patience and understanding will be to take a deep breath and think "patience" to herself.

INSTRUCTIONS FOR PRACTICING THE PRESENCE OF LOVE

This application includes both an extended and a brief practice.

1. Focus your intention to experience the presence of love with around and within you.
2. Concentrate on the idea that love is within you right now as well as with you, surrounding you.
3. Attend to your experience as you concentrate; your thoughts, posture, emotional state, and sensations. Think about how you would speak, move, see things, and present yourself if love were around you and within you.
4. As your experience becomes more vivid, create a mental or physical cue for this state.
5. Continue to experience this as long as it is comfortable.
6. Reflect on the experience, and on how it differs from the way you usually experience life.
7. Several times throughout the day, evoke the cue and reexperience the sense of love within you and around you.

TIPS

For Extended Practice

Imagine that someone or something representing love is really there with you.

As you get a sense of this presence next to you, start to feel the presence of love within you as well.

Imagine that you are seeing with the eyes of love, speaking with the voice of love, and touching with the hands of love.

This practice can take a good deal of energy; if you get tired, go back to centering prayer.

During the reflection phase, allow your mind to create a cue that will reconnect you with the presence of love. This cue may be a physical sign, a mental image, or a mental word.

For Brief Practice

The most important hint is that you practice. The more frequently, the better.

Don't judge the results. Just accept them. Sometimes, when you remember the cue, you will feel a strong presence. Other times, you will feel a weak presence, or nothing at all. As you practice more, the experiences will become more perceptible.

Brian and Maria's Results from Practicing the Presence of Love

Brian has worked on practicing the presence of love for a couple of weeks. The first few days, he forgot to do the brief version, except for a couple of times at the end of the day. He was able to experience the presence of peace when he did the extended version. After a couple of days of forgetting to do the brief version, Brian set his watch so that it beeped every hour. He promised himself that every day for the following week he would do the brief exercise every time his watch beeped, or as soon as possible afterward.

Brian now feels as if the peaceful presence has taken on a life of its own. Sometimes, he feels peaceful spontaneously. He is turning on the news less often during his drive home from work. Once, while driving, someone had cut in front of him. Brian got angry and began to glare at the other driver. Suddenly, he had the strong impression that his monk friend was sitting in the passenger seat looking at him. Brian felt embarrassed at his angry reaction. He reflected that the other driver probably wasn't trying to offend him personally. It seemed like his monk friend was smiling peacefully at him, and he laughed as his anger and tension drained away. A little farther down the road Brian came to a stop sign. He waved the person on his left to go through first. Brian felt peaceful and happy inside.

Maria started with a lot of resolve to do the brief practice frequently. However, she forgot to do it completely the first day after doing the extended session, and she did not remember on the second day until the evening. She was frustrated, but remembered her teacher saying, *The brief version of practicing the presence of love is hard to remember at first. Remember to have patience with yourself. If you continue to practice the extended version, and set up specific times to do the brief version, then it will become a habit.*

Maria decided that she would practice before and after meals, and before and after driving. That gave her at least eight brief practice sessions per day, without interrupting any activities. After one week, Maria notices a difference. She feels that her days are going smoother. She is more patient with herself and those around her. One Saturday evening, she began to get upset with her children after telling them for what seemed like the thousandth time to pick up their toys. All the progress she had made earlier in accepting their messes seemed to disappear. She was just as frustrated as ever, and ready to start yelling.

Suddenly, she felt the now familiar presence of a patient, understanding mother cradling her. She realized that God was very patient with her. God had asked her far more than a thousand times to stop speaking angrily, and was still patient with her. Maria took a deep breath, and said "patience" to herself. She felt the understanding, patient presence of God flow into her. Instead of saying the angry words that had been on her lips, she called her children. After getting their attention, she said, "Mommy needs to get some help or she is going to get upset." She then picked up one of the toys and put it on the shelf. Immediately her children began to participate, and once they had gotten started, they were able to complete the task without further effort on her part.

OPENING TO LOVE

Because love is transcendent, it is beyond any description or experience. You can have a more full experience of love if you move beyond ideas and open yourself to its presence. It is important to have practiced centering prayer and practicing the presence of love before you try opening to a more transcendent experience of love. The first two techniques give your mind a concrete experience of what love is like. Your mind has something to start with, so that what you open to will be love and not something random.

Though you need to start with some ideas or images of love, the fact that you will be opening means that you will be moving beyond your ideas. You use the ideas to orient your mind in the proper direction, but then you have to let go of them.

As you practice opening to love, you may experience new or unusual ideas about love. You may also see intense images, experience sounds, sense movements, or feel strong emotions. None of these have any real meaning. Enjoy them if they occur, but do not take them to be accurate messages about love. When you are truly open to transcendent love, your thinking mind is not active. It may experience things passively, but it is not processing them.

Since your thinking mind is not processing thoughts and images, you may have some ideas or images about love that do not make sense. This is a normal result. All the ideas, images, and feelings that occur during the experience are just side effects of what is, in essence, a completely spiritual experience.

So, let the ideas, images, and feelings come, but use the skills that you have developed during the attending practices to disengage from them throughout the execution phase of the session. It is during the reflection phase of the exercise that you should think about the ideas, images, and feelings that you experienced. During the reflection phase, your experiences are fresh in your memory and your thinking mind is active. Reflecting on the experiences you had during the execution phase will help you to make sense of them, and to integrate them into your current understanding.

Opening to love can induce a radically altered state of consciousness. This does not always happen, but you need to prepare for the possibility of its occurrence. Make sure that you set aside enough time for the session, so that you will be able to reorient yourself fully before you have to do anything else. This is not a technique that you should practice on your lunch hour at work, or just before driving somewhere. Set aside twenty to thirty minutes for practicing the technique, but make sure that you will have another thirty or so minutes afterward before you have to do anything active or stressful.

Do not use this as the only spirituality exercise you practice. You should spend at least as much time in either centering prayer or the extended version of practicing the presence of love as you do in opening to love. That means that you will practice opening to love once per week or less. Since you will practice it infrequently, you can schedule it for a weekend or other day that is not too busy. Early morning or evening are good times to practice.

The opening to love technique is quite simple. You first focus on your intention to experience complete, transcendent love. Of course, no one knows exactly what this is like, but you make it your intention anyway. Then, you concentrate on the experiences of love that you have had from centering prayer or practicing the presence of love. The stronger and clearer that you are able to concentrate on those experiences, the better.

After concentrating on the experiences of love that you have had so far, simply do an opening technique. As you experience the vastness and space that come with opening, recall your experiences of love from time to time. That is all there is to it.

Brian's Experience with Opening to Love

Brian has been having consistent success with practicing the presence of love. He is now beginning a session of opening to love. It is early on a Sunday morning. He usually doesn't practice on Sunday, but he skipped Saturday's meditation session because he would be less busy today.

Brian sits comfortably, closes his eyes, and focuses his intention to experience transcendent love and peace. He doesn't quite know what this means, and wonders if he is doing it correctly. He remembers, *When you focus your intention for this exercise, you usually won't start with a complete idea of what you are trying to achieve.*

Simply be aware of your intention and then clarify it by concentrating on the experiences of peace and love that you have had.

Brian identifies his thoughts about making sure he does the exercise "right" as his usual obsessiveness, and disengages from them. He concentrates on recalling the feeling of peace that he has around and inside himself when he does the extended version of practicing the presence of love. After a couple of minutes, he senses the familiar presence of peace.

Brian imagines that he is on a mountaintop. He imagines the experience of vastness as he sits above everything. He then concentrates on the presence of peace being with him there. He opens to the experience of vastness, and imagines the peace filling it. Everywhere he looks, there is peace. As the presence of peace grows in immensity and intensity, Brian feels that he is floating upward off the mountaintop. He feels that he is floating in an atmosphere of peace. His body absorbs the peace, and it expands and contracts.

Soon, Brian is aware only of peace. He is only vaguely aware of his body. There are no colors, images, thoughts, or even emotions. He is just aware of a presence that is completely at peace. He is not sure if he is that presence, or if the presence is of another; nor does it matter.

After a period of timelessness, Brian feels his awareness of his body returning. He struggles against it a bit, but remembers the advice of his teacher, *The amount of time you can spend in the open state will be limited. Often, your body starts getting restless after about twenty minutes. It is important to accept that without fighting it. The open state is quite enjoyable, but you can't force it. If you start to get restless and find yourself coming out of it, just accept that and allow your state of consciousness to return gradually to normal. You can't stay in that state and live your life. The purpose of this exercise is to move into a state in which you experience a connection with a spiritual presence. Then you must use the other techniques to bring that presence more noticeably into your daily life.*

Brian reluctantly accepts the need to return from the experience. He feels his body resting on the pillow and remembers the day and his surroundings. He reflects on the experience for a few minutes. He notices a desire to repeat this as often as possible, but he remembers a warning from his teacher. *Be careful about becoming addicted to experiences. The purpose of this exercise is to give you a deeper experience of spiritual presence. But there is much more to spirituality than that. You need to bring this spiritual presence into your life, and use it to touch the world around you. That is why you must practice one of the other spiritual applications, and do this exercise no more than once per week.*

Brian takes several minutes to reorient fully to his body, the time, and the surroundings. He feels quite relaxed and happy. He notices that twenty-five minutes have gone by since he began the exercise. Since the morning is still young, he decides to take an easy walk before breakfast.

Maria's Experience with Opening to Love

Maria is starting a session of opening to love. It is the third time that she is trying the exercise. The first two times were not very satisfying. She did not get quiet inside, and had lots of chaotic visual imagery. She and her teacher had discussed the problem. It turned out that Maria was expecting to have specific visual experiences. She expected to see white light, and she expected to see God as a person, probably wearing a robe. Maria had to struggle a bit before she could let go of these expectations. Her teacher was quite firm: *When you open to love, you go beyond any limiting images or thoughts. You do not reject them, but you realize that they do not show the complete reality of love. Love is infinite, and any image is quite finite. Your mind is too honest to let you get trapped by any stereotyped image. Concentrate on the ideas you have experienced of patience and love. That is as close as your thinking mind can come to the infinite reality of love. Then, open up to that, and disengage from any othr experiences as distractions.*

Maria starts by focusing her intention to experience God's love in a transcendent way. She then relaxes and concentrates on the presence of love and patience that she is familiar with from practicing the presence of love. After a few minutes, she experiences the feeling of being cradled by a loving, patient, understanding, motherly presence. Maria then uses the opening technique of feeling her body expand as she inhales and contract as she exhales.

While feeling her body expand and contract, Maria focuses from time to time on the patient, understanding presence around her. As she continues, she feels her awareness of her body change. She does not know quite where her body ends. Maria sees colors and shapes float past her. She starts trying to form the shapes into the image that she thinks would be appropriate, the image of a person surrounded by white light. This seems difficult and the image does not form. Maria then hears the firm voice of her teacher, *Do not try to make any particular image appear. Do not hold on to any image that arises. Simply concentrate on what you have experienced of patience and love, and continue to open to that. Any images that appear in this technique are just traps for your mind, so stay disengaged from them.*

Maria realizes that she is getting hooked on her expectation, so she reminds herself of her intention and disengages from trying to make the image of a person in white light appear. She concentrates again on the experience of patience and love surrounding her, and feels her body expand and contract. The colors and shapes return, but only briefly. Then, she feels like she is becoming bigger and bigger, with nothing but patience and love inside her. She continues to feel as if she is growing, spreading out to cover a huge area. All the while, there is nothing but patience and love within her.

While she experiences this, images arise and disappear. Maria finds that if she focuses too much on an image, then she loses some of the strength of the feeling of love and patience. So she just notices the images and stays disengaged from them, concentrating instead on the idea of peace and love. After a period of time—she is not certain how long—Maria feels her normal body awareness returning. She allows herself to reorient slowly, remembering the day, the time, and her surroundings.

As she reflects on her experience, she realizes that she doesn't remember much, except being in a state of peace and love that permeated her whole being. Maria realizes that she still feels disoriented. She wiggles her fingers and toes, and then flexes her arms and legs. She feels quite peaceful, patient, and loving. She takes her time getting up, and then does some quiet activities around the house for a little while.

INSTRUCTIONS FOR OPENING TO LOVE

Transcendent love is beyond our ability to comprehend logically. Spaciousness lets us go beyond our logical limitations to experience love more deeply.

1. Focus your intention to open to the experience of love.
2. Concentrate on the experiences of love you have had in either centering prayer or practicing the presence of

love. The experiences from practicing the presence of love are usually the clearest and easiest to concentrate on.

3. Do an opening technique (either of the following can be used).

   Imagine being in a vast open space, like the top of a mountain. Imagine that love is surrounding you and fills the vastness in every direction, as far as you can perceive.

   Feel your body expanding and contracting as you breathe. Then imagine that love is filling the space that is expanding and contracting.
4. Disengage from any images or thoughts, and go back to concentrating on love filling the space. Keep opening more and more.
5. When you feel restless or your alarm signals you, stop and reflect on the experience.
6. Reorient yourself slowly and thoroughly. Remember the time, the surroundings, and stretch your body gently before you get up.

TIPS

Feel as if the presence of love is going deeper and deeper inside of you.

Feel as if there is more and more space inside you, and it is being filled with love.

Variability in experience is common, both within the session and between sessions.

Your perception of the experience is not an accurate measure of its benefit to your spirit.

If you are experiencing distractions, it is important to simply return to feeling the presence of love, and then to open to it again. Your spirit can benefit even when your conscious mind is caught up with distractions, as long as you continue to disengage from the distractions and attempt to continue the practice.

When coming back, it is important to reorient to the normal waking state thoroughly. It can help to eat a light snack afterward.

Brian and Maria's Results from Opening to Love

Brian has practiced opening to love every Sunday for three weeks. His experiences in the last two sessions were not as powerful as those in the first session. He was a little disappointed, but his teacher had emphasized that the images and perceptual changes were not an accurate reflection of the benefit received from the technique.

Brian is noticing that he feels a connection with other people and the world that is quite peaceful. This feeling of peace is often quite faint, but it is gradually growing stronger. It is a welcoming of the presence of the other living things in the world. It is also an understanding that the earth, sky, wind, cloud, sun, and rain are also living and interconnected in some way. Brian can sense how he often acts and presents himself forcefully as he goes through his day. This clashes with the sense of peaceful connectedness. He realizes that much of his forcefulness is unnecessary, so he is acting more gently as he moves and speaks. He can be firm if he has to, but he need not be forceful all the time. As he deepens this experience of peaceful connection, his environment seems to respond, and people act more peacefully in his presence.

After her sessions of opening to love, Maria retains a feeling of joy and peace for several hours. She wanted to practice more frequently, but her teacher warned her against it: *Opening to love can be very enjoyable, but you must practice the other spirituality applications in order to keep from getting too spaced-out. If you don't stay grounded, you won't be much use to anyone.* She practices three times in the next month. At the end of that month, she feels more serene. She can stay calm and peaceful, even when things are not going the way she wants. She has a faith that things are really all right, and she doesn't need to be in control of them all the time. Her feeling of being in the presence of patience and love is more palpable, and she shows much more patience with those around her. This has a calming effect on the emotional atmosphere in her home and at work.

CONCLUSION

The three spirituality applications we have described are the most important applications in this book. Inner peace requires more than health, prestige, or even good relationships with others. We all need a sense of connection with love beyond our human existence. You will get that from practicing the spirituality applications.

These three applications build on each other when practiced in sequence. Centering prayer trains your mind to focus on something quite abstract, the idea of love. This prepares it to concentrate on that idea, and to create a vivid experience of it in practicing the presence of love. Once you have the experience of feeling love within and around you, you can direct your intention clearly enough in opening to love.

The brief version of practicing the presence of love is the most important of all the brief applications in this book. It will allow you to maintain a close connection with love, no matter what is going on around you. It is a superb antidote to the pressures of modern life. You should practice it daily, and preferably several times each day.

twelve

conclusion: Integrating Meditation into Daily Life

This precious human life is worth more than a wish-fulfilling gem. You only gain its like the once. So hard to get, so easily destroyed . . . Use it well.

Tsongkapa

By following the instructions outlined in this book, you will have acquired a system that allows you to find peace in your daily life. You will have learned basic techniques to develop your mental qualities, and applications to improve your health, enhance your performance, strengthen your relationships, and deepen your spirituality.

Now, you need to integrate these activities into your life in a balanced way. We have introduced sixteen techniques in this book. Obviously, you cannot practice all of them regularly, unless you are going to spend a lot more than ninety minutes per week meditating. You must rotate through the techniques systematically, so that you can continue to improve in a balanced manner.

The basic techniques develop the primary mental qualities. It is important to keep practicing them. You should spend thirty minutes per week practicing an extended basic meditation technique: an attending, concentrating, or opening technique. You need not practice an extended centering technique because you will gain the benefits of that from concentrating. If you practice one basic technique per week, rotating through the three basic extended techniques in three weeks, it will be sufficient to keep honing your mental qualities.

Spend the rest of your extended sessions practicing applications. The applications to spirituality are the most important; a deep spiritual connection is most closely associated with inner peace. Practice extended spirituality techniques for thirty minutes per week. Alternate between opening to love and either centering prayer or practicing the presence of love.

If you plan to spend the minimum amount of ninety minutes per week doing extended sessions, this will leave thirty minutes per week for the other three areas: health, performance, and relationships. That is not enough time to work on all of them at once, but you can spend one or more weeks working on one area, then move to another, and still make progress. Of course, if you spend more time meditating, you will be able to work on more applications.

As important as the extended techniques are, the brief techniques are even more important for integrating meditation into your daily life. With persistence, you will easily be able to do ten to fifteen brief techniques during the course of the day. These brief practice sessions will give you a tremendous opportunity to maintain your skills and improve your application of them.

The most important of all the brief techniques is the short version of practicing the presence of love. You should do this at least several times per day. Just after waking and just before sleeping are two good times for it. Brief versions of autonomic relaxation or inner harmony can be used frequently to relieve stress. Even the brief centering technique of "calm—relaxed" can be used in this way. For times when you feel especially stressed, use the brief opening technique to get some mental space.

To keep up your basic skills, you should practice the brief attending and concentrating techniques on alternating days of the week. If you are working on improving a relationship, then practice building positive energy for a minute at a time, several times per day. If you are focusing on improving your performance at a specific task, then practice a short version of directed imagination several times per day. By making a habit of practicing the brief techniques, you will be able to progress rapidly without taking time away from important activities.

A summary of the techniques covered in this book follows. The durations and frequencies that we suggest are based on the minimum of ninety minutes per week of extended sessions. If you spend more time than that doing extended sessions, then you can do more than the minimums that we list. Please remember that each technique starts with focusing your intention and ends with reflecting on your experience.

BASIC PRACTICES

CENTERING

Definition—Maintaining continuous awareness of a physical or mental object. The object you maintain awareness of is called your center.

Purpose—Develops mental steadiness and prepares you to do the more advanced techniques of attending and concentrating.

Extended Technique—Focus on the sensations in your lower abdomen. If you get distracted, return your awareness to those sensations.

Brief Technique—Focus on a simple mental phrase such as "calm—relaxed" or "calm—alert" for up to thirty seconds.

Continued Practice—Not needed. You may use the brief technique for stress reduction during the day.

ATTENDING

Definition—Identifying and disengaging from sensations, thoughts, and emotions.

Purpose—Develops mental pliancy and warmth.

Extended Technique—Focus on the sensations of air moving at the entrance of your nostrils. Identify and disengage from any distractions.

Brief Technique—Observe the sensations, thoughts, and feelings that are going through your mind. Spend only ten to twenty seconds recalling your experience of the preceding couple of minutes.

Continued Practice—Do the extended technique for a total of thirty minutes every third week. Rotate this with concentrating and opening. Do the brief technique two or three times every other day.

CONCENTRATING

Definition—Maintaining intense awareness of a mental object and perceiving it in complete detail without being distracted.

Purpose—Develops mental steadiness and clarity.

Extended Technique—Concentrate on the memory of a simple shape, a simple sound, or a simple movement.

Brief Technique—Concentrate for one to two minutes on the memory of an event that occurred earlier in the day.

Continued Practice—Do the extended technique for a total of thirty minutes every third week. Rotate with attending and opening. Do the brief technique two or three times every other day.

OPENING

Definition—Letting go of how the mind organizes reality, so that a different organization can arise.

Purpose—Develops mental spaciousness.

Extended Technique 1—Imagine being in a wide-open place, such as on a mountaintop. Imagine that everything is very far away and feel your mind filling the vastness.

Extended Technique 2—Feel your chest and abdomen expand as you inhale and contract as you exhale. Imagine that your whole body is expanding and contracting as you breathe in and out.

Brief Technique—Take a deep breath and imagine it filling your whole body with space. As you breathe out, imagine that the space is surrounding you and everything else is moving farther away.

Continued Practice—Do one of the extended techniques for a total of thirty minutes every third week. Rotate with attending and concentrating. Do the brief technique as needed, whenever you feel especially stressed.

HEALTH APPLICATIONS

AUTONOMIC RELAXATION

Uses centering and attending.

Purpose — Relaxes several parts of the autonomic nervous system, enhancing the natural healing powers of the body.

Continued Practice — Practice going through the technique in two minutes, and do this a couple of times per day for stress reduction.

INNER HARMONY

Uses attending and concentrating.

Purpose — Creates a more positive relationship between mind and body, which facilitates greater harmony among the body's systems.

Continued Practice — Practice going through the technique in progressively less time, until you can feel results within a couple of minutes. Then do it a couple of times per day for stress-reduction.

HEALING LIGHT

Uses attending, concentrating, and opening.

Purpose — Creates an altered state of consciousness directed by the intention for healing. This allows the mind to find indirect paths to a healthier state.

Continued Practice — Not needed, unless you are working on a specific health issue, in which case it can be done up to twice per day.

PERFORMANCE APPLICATIONS

HEIGHTENED FOCUS

Uses centering and attending.

Purpose – Allows you to enter a state in which you are calm, alert, and focused on everything pertinent to doing your task, while ignoring everything that is irrelevant.

Continued Practice – Use this to improve at any task.

DIRECTED IMAGINATION

Uses attending and concentrating.

Purpose—Lets you experience successful events in your imagination, so that you are better able to do them when you need to.

Continued Practice—Do the extended version until you can effortlessly imagine the successful event. Then, recall that briefly several times during the day. This is not needed unless you are working on improving at a specific task.

CLEARING BLOCKS

Uses attending, concentrating, and opening.

Purpose—Helps you to overcome inner blocks to success. These blocks may come from prior events, or from pursuing goals that are not right for you.

Continued Practice—Use this if you are having difficulty with directed imagination, especially if directed imagination has stopped working.

RELATIONSHIP APPLICATIONS

BUILDING POSITIVE ENERGY

Uses centering and attending.

Purpose—Restores your awareness of the positive aspects of a relationship.

Continued Practice—Do this for one to two minutes daily, even if your relationship is going well. Do one minute sessions several times a day for any relationship you are working on.

CLOSENESS DURING CONFLICT

Uses attending and concentrating.

Purpose—Enables you to have dialogue about a difficult issue with another person, without avoiding what you need to say, and without getting overwhelmed by emotions. It often gives you insight into what makes the issue difficult.

Continued Practice—Not needed, unless there is an issue you need to work on.

SPACE WITHOUT DISTANCE

Uses attending, concentrating, and opening.

Purpose—Allows to you to feel that you have the space necessary for personal growth, without feeling that you have to physically or emotionally distance yourself from others.

Continued Practice—Use this if you feel trapped or closed in by a relationship. It is also a good idea to use this once a month or so, even if things are going well.

SPIRITUALITY APPLICATIONS

CENTERING PRAYER

Uses centering and attending.

Purpose—Places your mind in a state that is receptive to love, while allowing you to disengage from distractions.

Continued Practice—Use this or the extended version of practicing the presence of love for thirty minutes every other week.

PRACTICING THE PRESENCE OF LOVE

Uses attending and concentrating.

Purpose—Creates a vivid experience of love within and around you, and trains your mind to recall that experience quickly in response to a cue.

Continued Practice—Use this or the extended version of centering prayer for thirty minutes every other week. Do the brief version of this technique several times every day.

OPENING TO LOVE

Uses attending, concentrating, and opening.

Purpose—Allows your mind to experience love in a way that transcends logical limitations.

Continued Practice—Practice this technique for thirty minutes every other week. Alternate this application with either centering prayer or practicing the presence of love.

HINTS ON WHEN TO DO BRIEF TECHNIQUES

- before and after meals
- just after waking up, unless you are about to do an extended session
- just before falling asleep, unless you have just finished an extended session
- while walking from one room to another
- while walking out to the car
- before or after driving
- while someone else is driving
- while going to the bathroom
- while washing up after going to the bathroom
- in the shower
- while on hold during a telephone call
- before picking up the newspaper or a magazine
- instead of picking up the newspaper or a magazine
- before or after reading a book about meditation

BRIAN'S RESULTS

Brian is sitting down to lunch with his sister, Karen. After exchanging the usual pleasantries, Brian reaches across the table and hands Karen a small, gift-wrapped box. Karen opens it and finds a heart-shaped pendant on a gold chain. She pauses in surprise, and then looks at Brian, smiling. "Brian, it's beautiful. Thank you so much. But what is it for?"

"I wanted to thank you for your suggestion about a year ago. About meditation."

"You've kept at it, haven't you?"

"Yes, and I'm real glad I did. I'm doing better in a lot of ways."

"That's great, Brian. The family has noticed a lot of positive changes, too. You are a lot less forceful, a lot less stressed, and yet still focused when you need to be."

"I feel better mentally and physically, and I'm a lot more peaceful."

"Are you going to keep meditating?"

"Of course. It took awhile, but I was able to achieve the goals that I set for myself, so why not keep going."

"What are you going to work on now?"

"Well, I can't do everything at once."

"No, otherwise all that peace will disappear."

"That's right. I want to continue the applications for bringing a greater sense of peace into my life, and focus on increasing that at home. So that will be an ongoing project. While I'm doing that, I plan to work on getting into better physical shape. That's a good health goal, and I should reach it after a couple of months. My relationship goal is to improve my interactions with my coworkers, and my performance goal is to increase my efficiency at work. I'll probably alternate between those two for several months."

"Sounds like you have things carefully planned out."

"Well, progress will take some time, but the time is going to pass anyway, so I might as well do something with it."

"I'm glad your doing this, Brian."

"Me too. And thanks, again."

MARIA'S RESULTS

Maria and her friend Susan are taking a walk together after dinner. Susan says, "It was very nice of you to treat me to dinner, Maria. Thank you very much."

"Oh, my pleasure," Maria replied. "Besides, I owe you a lot for suggesting that I take up meditation."

"It has made a difference, hasn't it?"

"Definitely. Instead of demands, I have challenges. As I deal with them, I feel like I am moving forward. I'm becoming a better person."

"What do you like best of what has happened?"

"Hmm . . . well my relationship with God has gotten much deeper. It's gotten far more complex and more personal than I ever thought it could be."

"That sounds good."

"There is a whole feminine side to God that I'm discovering. It's something I can relate to as a woman, and God can relate to me as a woman, too."

"Beautiful! Anything else?" Susan queried.

"Well, I'm going to continue working on my spiritual life, but I also have some new goals."

"Really? Go on," Susan encouraged.

"I'd like to lose some weight, and I think that would be a good health goal. But you know, before I work on that, I'd like to start playing tennis. So I'll focus on using meditation to help myself learn tennis, and then I'll use meditation to help myself lose weight."

"Very good."

"And things are going well at home. After I reach a healthier weight, I plan on increasing the warmth and affection I have with my husband, Kevin. So that will be my new relationship goal."

"Those sound great, Maria"

"You know something? I really wish Kevin would do this too. He is quite supportive and appreciates the changes that I've made, but he doesn't practice himself. Meditation would really help him."

"That's true, but the best way to get him interested is to keep up your own practice. As your life becomes more peaceful, he will get more interested."

"So I shouldn't try to talk him into it?"

"Exactly. But you can encourage him when he shows interest in what is clearly helping you."

"I get it. Like the way you told me about meditation a year ago."

"That's right."

"I see. Thanks, Susan."

suggested reading

While there are numerous books on meditation that have shaped our thinking, a number can be considered primary influences, and we have listed these below. Some of the translations that we have used are out of print, and we have done our best to list other translations or versions that are available. Those listed that are out of print can usually be obtained through libraries.

Anonymous. *Advice from a Spiritual Friend*. (Boston: Wisdom Publications, 1996).

Anonymous. *The Cloud of Unknowing and The Book of Privy Counseling*. Translated by William Johnston. (Garden City, NY: Image Books, 1973).

Assagioli, Roberto. *Psychosynthesis*. (New York: Viking, 1965; out of print).

Bennett, Bruce M., Donald D. Hoffman, and Chetan Prakash. *Observer Mechanics: A Formal Theory of Perception*. (San Diego: Academic Press, 1989; out of print).

Hayward, Jeremy W. *Perceiving Ordinary Magic: Science and Intuitive Wisdom*. (Boulder: New Science Library, 1984).

His Holiness the Dalai Lama. *The Good Heart: A Buddhist Perspective on the Teachings of Jesus*. (Boston: Wisdom Publications, 1996).

Pabongka Rinpoche. *Liberation in the Palm of Your Hand.* (Boston: Wisdom Publications, 1997).

St. John of the Cross. *Dark Night of the Soul.* Translated by E. Allison Peers. (Garden City, NY: Image Books, 1959).

St. Teresa of Avila. *Interior Castle.* Translated by E. Allison Peers. (Garden City, NY: Image Books, 1972).

St. Teresa of Avila. *The Way of Perfection.* Translated by E. Allison Peers. (Garden City, NY: Image Books, 1991).

Thera, Nyanaponika. *The Heart of Buddhist Meditation.* (York Beach, ME: Samuel Weiser, 1988).

Welwood, John. *Awakening the Heart: East/West Approaches to Psychotherapy and the Healing Relationship.* (Boulder: New Science Library, 1983).

Wilber, Ken, and others. *Transformations of Consciousness.* (Boston: New Science Library, , 1986).

Yeshe, Lama Thubten. *Introduction to Tantra: A Vision of Totality.* (Boston: Wisdom Publications, 1993).